POPE FRANCIS' PROFOUND PERSONALISM AND POVERTY

POPE FRANCIS' PROFOUND PERSONALISM AND POVERTY

Rev. Robert E. Lauder

Resurrection Press
An Imprint of
CATHOLIC BOOK PUBLISHING CORP.
Totowa • New Jersey

First published in February, 2017
Catholic Book Publishing/Resurrection Press
77 West End Road
Totowa, NJ 07512

ISBN 978-1-933066-19-6

Cover photo by Aristide Economopoulos-Pool/Getty Images used with permission.

Printed in the United States of America

www.catholicbookpublishing.com

1 2 3 4 5 6 7 8 9 10

Acknowledgments

Grateful acknowledgement is made
to *The Brooklyn Tablet* for
material which appeared previously in its pages;
to Emilie Cerar of Resurrection Press,
whose guidance and encouragement
in bringing the book to publication
have been greatly appreciated;
and to my dear friend Iris Flores,
whose assistance and expertise
helped to make this book possible.

Dedication

This book is dedicated to
Regina
whose courage and love
have been a blessing and inspiration in my life,
and in the lives of many.

Contents

INTRODUCTION 9

CHAPTER ONE
The Pope's Interview 21

CHAPTER TWO
Apostolic Exhortation: "The Joy of the Gospel" 37

CHAPTER THREE
Insights from Personalism 47

CHAPTER FOUR
A Revolution of Love 57

CHAPTER FIVE
Consumerism: The Objectification of Persons 77

CHAPTER SIX
A Most Important Encyclical 93

CHAPTER SEVEN
Mercy 111

CONCLUSION 127

Introduction

This book is not intended as a scholarly presentation of Pope Francis' thought. Nor is it presented as a scholarly analysis of the philosophy of personalism. Rather, it is an attempt at sharing how and why Pope Francis' insights have inspired me and, I am certain, countless others. The book is personal, very much a presentation of my reactions and enthusiasm for Pope Francis, but I hope not private. It represents an attempt at reflecting on Pope Francis' insights and emphases in the hope that my reflections will help readers appreciate more fully the Pope's vision, and so live the Gospel with the joy that the Holy Father encourages. Francis' insights into the human person are profound, exciting, and inspiring. Never does the Holy Father speak or write about the mystery of person from an ivory tower removed from the day-to-day struggles that are part and parcel of every person's life. Francis' faith illuminates his own understanding of personal existence and his faith challenges us, not only to reflect deeply on who we are, but to incorporate into our lives, as honestly and courageously as we can, the most profound meaning of the mysteries of God, self, and neighbor. While the philosophy of personalism presents beautiful, almost mystical, insights into personal existence, Francis relentlessly, but lovingly, challenges our consciences and urges us to live differently, to incarnate personalist insights into our relationships with God and with others.

Two Types of Poverty

It is almost impossible to read a story about Pope Francis that does not mention that he emphasizes the needs of the poor. Many religious leaders have spoken about the poor, about our obligation to be concerned about the poor and to help them, but somehow Pope Francis' message seems to be having a special impact. The attractiveness and appeal of the Pope seem to help greatly in conveying his message. I believe that one way to enter more deeply into the Holy Father's vision of humanity is to reflect on two meanings of poverty that shed light on Francis' profound understanding of human nature, on his grasp of world problems, and how to solve those problems.

One meaning of poverty I describe as poverty in being, the other I call poverty in having. Every human person is poor in being. To be finite is to be fragile and limited. We are fragile physically, psychologically, and spiritually. None of us is God. We have no choice about being poor in being. This is how we find ourselves; this is how God made us. We are created for a loving relationship with God, and with our brothers and sisters, and nothing less will fulfill us. On this side of heaven not even those loving relationships will totally fulfill us.

Poverty in having is not to have sufficient goods and possessions to live a decent human life. One third of the human race is poor in having. Because that portion of the human race does not have enough to eat, many are starving to death. Billionaires are not poor in having. It may be that some billionaires are so rich, they do not even know how much money they have. However, on the level of being, billionaires are as poor, as fragile, and as finite as the rest of us. If a billionaire does not know that he or she is as poor in being as the rest of us, that person's life might turn out to be a spiritual disaster. Such a person might implicitly think they are "quasi-divine," in no need of any kind of help from anyone, including God. Such a person might not believe that he or she needs redemption. In her novel *Wise Blood*, Flannery O'Connor satirized this view when she had the main character, Hazel Motes, announce, "Nobody with a good car needs to be justified. . ." [1]

Perhaps one reason that Jesus talks so much in Scripture about the "poverty in having" is that the experience of physical poverty might help them to be aware of how needy they are in being. I suspect that this is one reason that members of religious orders take vows of poverty. The vow of poverty should free those who take it from any inordinate attachment to possessions. For those who take a vow of poverty, the illusion that our society promotes, namely that things are going to free us, save us, and redeem us, that our value as persons can be seen by what we possess, should be exposed as an illusion.

Reflecting on our poverty in being can help us see more deeply into God's love for us. Not one of us had the right to be created. Each one of us is created from nothing by God's love. All of creation is a product of Divine

---

[1] Flannery O'Connor, *Wise Blood*, (New York: The Noonday Press, Farrar, Straus and Giroux, 1949), p. 113.

Love. When God loves, being appears. I am reminded of philosopher Frederick Wilhelmsen's wonderful insight: *"What being loved makes being do, is precisely be."* [2] Every second of our lives, God's love keeps us in existence. The crucifixion of Jesus is the great sign of God's love. The Son of God identified with us even unto death. Divine providence surrounds us because of God's love for us.

Pope Francis, both in talks and in writing, often focuses on poverty in having. He continually reminds us of the enormous physical and material needs that countless numbers of people have. The Pope's concern and compassion are almost palpable. He *really* cares. In addition to his explicit references to poverty in having, the Holy Father's message is always at least implicitly about poverty in being. Francis wants us to know ourselves and to know others more deeply; and to love others, as well as ourselves, more deeply. He wants us to think and to love under the light provided by Jesus' death and resurrection.

Danger of Discouragement

I am saddened every time I hear that large numbers of Catholics have stopped attending Mass regularly. Somehow the truths that the Church teaches about the celebration of the Eucharist are not appreciated by many. How could anyone, who believes that the Risen Christ is offering Himself to the Father at every Eucharist and that those present can receive the Risen Christ, not attend Mass regularly?

---

[2] Frederick D. Wilhelmsen, *The Metaphysics of Love*, (New York: Transaction Publishers, 1962), p. 139.

Reflecting on our poverty in being can help us to see how the virtue of hope dictates our way of relating to God. I agree completely with St. Paul that love is the greatest of the three virtues, but the longer I live, the more I appreciate how important hope is. We are called to place our trust, our very lives in the loving embrace of God. We do not save or redeem ourselves. We are saved and redeemed by the Incarnate God's life, death, and resurrection. Nothing is more powerful than God's love for us. Nothing! Pope Francis tells us this profound truth, at least implicitly, in everything he writes and every time he speaks.

Not long ago, I had an exceptionally interesting experience in a class at St. John's University. I was trying to help students prepare for an exam and so I decided to read aloud some pages from the text we were using in the course and see if the students understood what I was reading and whether they had any questions. The section in the text we were using was about the mystery of love. I have read and studied the section many times, but as I was reading it to the students, something strange happened. Insights that I had received from the text many times previously, seemed to leap off the page at me, and though I was more than slightly familiar with the insights, they seemed new in some strange way, as though I was grasping them for the first time or at least seeing more deeply into them than I had previously. As I was having this experience, I wondered what the students thought. I could not tell if they were grasping the insights that I found so exciting.

All the insights focused on the mystery of person and how a human is a unique being in our experience. What makes the person so different from material things in our experience and even from animals we encounter is that a human person's nature is to be relational. There are various ways of articulating this. I like expressions such as to be human is "to be relational," "to be open to others," "to be present to others," "to be in dialogue with others." Wherever a human being is, that person is in relation. This is because of human consciousness, which is relational. It is impossible just to be conscious. Human consciousness is always consciousness *of*. We can decide *how* we will relate, but not *whether* we will relate. God has made us relational beings. The most dynamic, outgoing, lively extrovert is relational; the most lethargic, withdrawn, shy introvert is relational. *The Baltimore Catechism* was implicitly calling attention to the relational essence of the human person in its statement that we were made to know and love God in this life, and to be happy with God forever in the next. Francis is trying to help us to expand our notion of relationship. We are related, not just to those in our immediate experience. The Holy Father stresses that we have brothers and sisters around the world. He wants our consciences to expand and deepen.

My philosophical view of the human person is that each person is on a journey highlighted by knowing and loving, and that each act of knowing and loving can help a person to become aware, to some extent, of three mysteries: the mystery of self, the mystery of other persons, and the mystery of God. No truth that we come to know is ever the final truth. We cannot stop asking questions. This is because our minds are magnetized toward God and no truth less than the Divine Truth

Who is God will ever satisfy us. If our desire to know goes unhindered and unblocked, the ultimate goal is the affirmation of God. No love is ever the final love because no finite good is big enough or good enough, to satisfy our capacity to love. Once again, if our love is not restricted or distracted, or in some way misled, then our love points toward an Absolute Good Who is God.

I find it interesting that some atheistic philosophers accept the basic sketch that I have offered of human knowing and loving. In that sense, they would agree that our knowing and loving, if they are to make sense, should be interpreted as pointing toward an Absolute Being whom people call God. However, these atheistic philosophers sadly report that they do not think there is any such being and so reality does not make sense. They conclude that because there is no God, reality is absurd. To put it simply: it would seem that everything in us points toward the existence of God, but the tragic joke is that there is no God and so a human being is a useless passion, a meaningless voyager in an absurd world.

I have mentioned that our knowing and loving, if not impeded, distracted, or restricted, point toward God. Of course, in our society they are impeded, distracted, and restricted. In recent years, I have come to see that much in our society not only does not encourage people to ask ultimate questions, but also, actually discourages such questioning. A very important task for the new evangelization is to help people ask those ultimate questions. Christians believe that there are answers to those questions, but does that matter if their contemporaries do not think the questions are important, or indeed, if they do not even think about such questions? In spite of my impression that our society is becoming more secular and many Catholics seem to have drifted away from the Church, I am not discouraged. Probably for many people directly involved in the new evangelization through some apostolate, at least occasionally, there can be a serious temptation to become discouraged. I know I have experienced that temptation often.

When a person is excited and enthusiastic about something and tries very hard to interest others but receives no encouragement, it is not easy to stay excited and enthusiastic. All of us like to see results. When we do not see them, we can be especially vulnerable. A young priest I know told me that his main criticism of the seminary education he received was that he was led to believe that after ordination if he did everything perfectly, people would respond. For example, if he ran a religious education program that was outstanding, people would respond. His experience was that some people did not respond to programs he organized and gave a great deal of time and energy to, and this experience tempted him to become discouraged. Why couldn't others see the value of what was the center of his life?

I think I was more prone to become discouraged when I was much younger. My attitude now is that those of us involved in a Christian apostolate should try to do our best, but then the rest is up to the Holy Spirit. We do not save or redeem people. Jesus does that. Also, no one can know how God is operative in someone's life, even in someone who to us may seem totally uninterested in God's existence and presence in his or her life. I love Pope Francis' conviction that God is part of everyone's life. If that conviction is true, and I am certain it is, how can we ever allow ourselves to be discouraged?

A short time ago, I made a retreat. I welcomed the opportunity to make the retreat because I thought I needed time to reflect on my life. To help me reflect I used a book that I had read several years ago when it was strongly recommended to me. The book is Sebastian Moore's *The Crucified Jesus Is No Stranger*.[3] When I first read the book, I found it very demanding. On this recent retreat, I still found it demanding, but perhaps the atmosphere of the retreat was a special aid because I found some of Moore's insights striking.

There is a lengthy paragraph in Moore's book, which I found both difficult and enlightening. Mentioning that there is something in the soul of the believer, which recognizes Jesus as the experience of that something, Moore asks what that something is and offers the following answer:

> *"It is the person's life, sensed—however obscurely—as hungry for some ultimate meaningfulness, convinced of some ultimate meaningfulness. It is the root of rare moments of an unaccountable happiness. It is what idealists and reformers draw upon. It is why there are idealists and reformers. It is a spark of the divine. It is what Augustine is talking about when he says 'Thou has made us for thyself, and our heart is restless till it rests in thee.' 'Our heart', in that statement, is 'this something.' God's destining us 'for himself' is, however obscurely, experienced as restlessness, and even more obscurely, as promise. There is promise in us. And*

---

[3] Sebastian Moore, *The Crucified Jesus Is No Stranger*, (Minneapolis, Minnesota: The Seabury Press, 1977), p. 116.

*this 'promise' is a promise of life. It has to do, not
with something we want to get, but with being ourselves without any inhibition. The greatest happiness possible, and the very definition of happiness,
is to be oneself without any inhibition. And Augustine is saying that we can only be this way 'in God'.
The recognition of Jesus as 'this' is the work of the
Holy Spirit in a person."* [4]

That the Holy Spirit breathes where he will, that the
Spirit accompanies every person at every moment is
the reason for our hope. When the apostolates in which
we are involved seem to be going well and people seem
to be deeply touched, the Holy Spirit is present; when
nothing in our apostolates seems to be going well and
no one seems to be influenced or affected, the Holy
Spirit is still present.

Augustine's insight that our hearts are restless until
they rest in the Lord is profoundly true and we should
never forget that only union with God will ultimately
fulfill us. When I think of God's complete commitment
to us, I am embarrassed that I would ever feel discouraged. The victory has been won by Christ's death and
resurrection. The powers of evil cannot win in a battle
with God. Rather than discouragement, a proper
response to our involvement in evangelization would
seem to be overwhelming joy that we participate in
God's life and can be used by the Spirit to help others.
This joy is central to Pope Francis' vision of the Church.
He believes that our joy is a great sign of God's presence
and that our joy will attract and influence people.

---

[4] Ibid., p. 18.

Discussion Questions

1. Why is Pope Francis so appealing to so many people?

2. In his papacy, what is Pope Francis' greatest accomplishment, in your opinion?

3. Do you think there is any area in which Pope Francis could do more?

4. What does the author mean by "two types of poverty"? Can you explain them?

5. Does anything in the contemporary Catholic Church discourage you?

6. What does it mean to say that we are "magnetized by God"?

7. Are people hungry for some ultimate meaningfulness?

8. Does the joy within Catholics attract people to the Church?

Chapter One

The Pope's Interview

I cannot recall any time that any Pope has spoken that caused as much discussion as the first official interview that Pope Francis gave. The interview took place in three meetings in August of 2013, but was not released until September in sixteen Jesuit magazines across the world. The interview was conducted in person by Father Antonio Spadaro, S.J., editor-in-chief of *La Civilta Cattolica*, the Italian Jesuit journal. The editorial teams of several Jesuit journals around the world prepared questions that were sent to Father Spadaro, who organized them for the interview.

In addition to hearing comments about the interview from many people I have spent time with since the interview, I have read several essays about the interview. One of the best was written by Father James Martin, S.J. Noting that when he read it he knew that the interview was "spiritual dynamite," Father Martin wrote the following:

> *"The Pope touched upon almost every area of concern for modern-day Catholics from the role of women, to the need for reform in the Vatican curia, to tensions between traditionalists and progres-*

sives; he also spoke about his own spiritual journey with great feeling and his own failings with brutal candor." [5]

In *America*, the Jesuit weekly in which the interview appeared, the editor, Father Matt Malone, S.J., wrote the following:

> *"Other popes have given interviews, of course, and while they have been insightful and often spirited, they have also been didactic and formal. I suspect that this interview, along with the pope's extended remarks on the return trip from Rio de Janeiro last July, represent a new genre of papal communication, one that is fraternal rather than paternal. A spirit of generosity, humility and dare I say, deep affection is evident in these pages. . . . Pope Francis speaks to us as our brother; his we actually means, 'we,' not 'I.'"* [6]

Father Malone has touched on some of the key elements in the interview, and I think that the interview provides evidence as to why so many Catholics have been enthusiastic about Pope Francis' papacy. However, I learned that not everyone was happy about the Pope's remarks. I asked a priest friend what he thought of the Pope, and he remarked, "He shoots from the hip." I think the comment meant that Francis answers questions too quickly, that perhaps he should be more careful in his statements because he might be misunderstood or even misquoted. Because some of the statements of the Pope are so striking, I can understand my friend's concern, but I have to believe that

---

[5] James Martin, *Time*, September 20, 2013, online.
[6] Matt Malone, *America*, September 30, 2013, p. 2.

the Pope, aware of the media coverage that his remarks will receive, says exactly what he wishes to say. I strongly encourage readers of this book to read his interview. New York Cardinal Timothy Dolan described the interview as a "breath of fresh air."

Francis: Prophet of Hope

Asked a question about the Church, Pope Francis emphasized that the Church is a community; that no one is saved alone, as an isolated individual. He said the following:

> *"And the church is the people of God on the journey through history, with joys and sorrows. Thinking with the church, therefore, is my way of being a part of this people. And all the faithful, considered as a whole, are infallible in matters of belief, and the people display this* infallibilitas *in credendo, this infallibility in believing, through a supernatural sense of the faith of all the people walking together. . . . When the dialogue among the people goes down this road and is genuine, then it is assisted by the Holy Spirit. . . . We should not even think therefore, that 'thinking with the church' means only thinking with the hierarchy of the church."* [7]

How Francis' papacy is leading the Church is both interesting and important. He has emphasized that we must never forget the poor. His statements about the poor have already disturbed my conscience and probably the consciences of many. It is easy to forget those who may not be part of our daily experience, but I do not think Francis is going to allow us to do that. Why

---

[7] Pope Francis, *America*, September 30, 2013, p. 2.

has this Pope had an impact on so many? One reason is that he appears to be a deeply compassionate human being.

God's Love for Sinners

Rereading the Pope's interview, I continue to find that Francis is giving me wonderful, insightful, and hope-filled advice about how I should be a priest and how I should relate to those I serve. I very much like the Pope's emphasis on mystery and on the profound truth that Catholic dogma and belief should lead us into the future with confidence and hope. Francis points out that if one is a restorationist and a legalist and wants everything safe and clear, then that person will be frustrated. No one can understand God completely, but because of God sending His Son among us, we can have a deep relationship with our Savior and Redeemer. Pope Francis said the following:

> *"Tradition and memory of the past must help us to have the courage to open up new areas to God. Those who today always look for disciplinarian solutions, those who long for an exaggerated doctrinal 'security,' those who stubbornly try to recover a past that no longer exists—they have a static and inward-directed view of things. In this way faith becomes an ideology among other ideologies."* [8]

Probably all of us, when dealing with profound mysteries, want what is being taught and proclaimed to be crystal clear, even when we are dealing with Christian faith. While Christian dogma is profoundly true, it can-

---

[8] Ibid., p. 32.

not be crystal clear because it deals with the greatest mystery of all, the mystery of God, and with another great mystery, the mystery of the human person. Pope Francis is telling us to have courage. What we believe about God's love for us should enable us to place ourselves in God's hands with hope. I know this is very important, even though for most of my life, I have found this difficult to do. I feel a little like St. Paul, who wrote that the good that he wanted to do, he did not do, and the evil that he did not want to do, he actually did. All of us are sinners, but the presence of God in our lives should free and liberate us to be people of hope. Pope Francis comes across as a person who has enormous confidence in God. He radiates Christian hope, and he can help us to be people of hope. For me, one of the most important remarks that he made in the interview is the following:

> *"I have a dogmatic certainty: God is in every person's life. God is in everyone's life. You can, you must try to seek God in every human life. Although the life of a person is a land full of thorns and weeds, there is always a space in which the good seed can grow. You have to trust God."* [9]

At some time in my training or in my ministry, I accepted the image that God left a person's life when the person committed a serious sin. The image led me to think that people who did not attend the Eucharist on Sundays, or were in second non-sacramental marriages, or had been unfaithful to their marriage vows as living without God's presence in their lives. The image I had was that somehow, such people had built a fence

---

[9] Ibid., p. 32.

around themselves keeping God out, and the only way that God would re-enter was through some dramatic conversion on the part of the person. I think that I went so far as to imagine that there was no point in a Catholic who had committed a serious sin even praying until that person went to confession. Reflecting now on the way I once thought about people "in sin," I see my previous thinking as a confused jumble of truths, half-truths and errors. Without being aware of it, I had slipped into a kind of legalism and had an image of God as primarily someone who gave us rules and laws.

What Pope Francis has helped me to see in a new way is that the goodness and love of God goes way beyond, in fact infinitely beyond, any image I have of God. While I believe that because of our freedom we can reject God's love, I also believe that God never stops loving us. Encouraged by Francis' statement that we should try to find God's presence in "every human life," I now am confident that if we look for God's presence in every human life, we will find that presence. Should people, who at this point in their lives think they should not receive the sacraments, still pray? Now that seems like a really pointless question to me. I am amazed that I once thought their prayers would not reach God.

Irreversible Insight

A number of my friends have mentioned to me that Pope Francis reminds them of Pope St. John XXIII. Parts of Francis' interview also made me think of John XXIII. That may be due to Pope Francis' sense of humor or his joy-filled attitude. It may be that when he said that we have to find God in the world, I thought immediately of the Second Vatican Council and some of the wonderful documents that emerged from that gathering. Reading and rereading Pope Francis' interview brought back memories of the excitement and enthusiasm that was stirred up almost daily among my friends and me during the Council. Statements by Pope Francis during the interview not only urge us to be committed to Christ but also remind us that there should be no turning away from the insights of the Council.

Channels of Grace

With Pope Francis encouraging us, we should be hopeful that we can make a difference in the world. Of course, there is evil in the contemporary world, but there is also a great deal of good. The Holy Spirit breathes in the contemporary world, and animated by that Spirit, the Church—that means all of us—can be channels of God's grace. Asked by the interviewer what the Second Vatican Council accomplished, Pope Francis said the following:

> *"Its fruits are enormous. Just recall the liturgy. The work of liturgical reform has been a service to the people as a rereading of the Gospel from a concrete historical situation. Yes, there are hermenutics of continuity and discontinuity, but one thing is clear: the dynamic of reading the Gospel, actualizing its message for today—which was typical of Vatican II—is absolutely irreversible. . . . In fact, there is a temptation to seek God . . . in the past or in a possible future. God is certainly in the past because we can see the footprints. And God is also*

in the future as a promise. But the 'concrete' God, so to speak, is today. For this reason, complaining never helps us find God. The complaints of today about how 'barbaric' the world is—these complaints sometimes end up giving birth within the church to desires to establish order in the sense of pure conservatism, as a defense. No: God is to be encountered in the world of today. God manifests himself in historical revelation, in history. Time initiates processes, and space crystallizes them. God is in history, in the processes." [10]

I became interested and involved in a small way in liturgical reform while I was a student in the major seminary. Twice I attended the national meeting of the Liturgical Conference, and these two meetings were among the most profound experiences I have had in my life. At that time, I believed that if the sacraments were celebrated in the vernacular there would be enormous changes in how Catholics understood the sacraments, celebrated the sacraments, and allowed the sacraments to influence their lives. I believed the sacraments would form and shape us, form and shape the way we think, and form and shape the way we live. Looking back on my hopes and dreams, I suspect that in some ways, I was naïve, but I think my basic insight was correct. The liturgical reforms already have had a great impact, and I think they will continue to influence deeply the lives of Catholics.

One of the statements of the Pope that I especially like is his comment that the dynamic of reading the Gospel and analyzing its message for today is irre-

---

[10] Ibid., p. 30.

versible. Pope Francis is saying that whether we like everything about the Council or dislike some of what has followed in its wake, relating the insights of the Gospel to the world is an insight that should never be rejected or forgotten. The insight is "irreversible." Noting that some people who wish to encounter God also want to verify God's presence by an empirical method, Pope Francis stresses that a person cannot meet God in that way. He said:

> *"A contemplative attitude is necessary: it is the feeling that you are moving along the good path of understanding and affection toward things and situations. Profound peace, spiritual consolation, love of God and love of all things in God—this is the sign that you are on this right path."* [11]

The Power of Art

I enjoy reading interviews with celebrities—at least sometimes. If the interviewee is an actor or actress whom I admire, I read hoping that the interview will reveal the person as someone to admire, not only on the stage or screen, but also in real life. Even more than interviews with celebrities from the entertainment world, I enjoy reading interviews with authors. I think that I am hoping the interview will reveal a new dimension that I might have missed in something that the author wrote. But the interview with the Pope is special. It can help us better understand Pope Francis and what his priorities as Pope might be.

I found one section of Pope Francis' interview espe-

[11] Ibid., p. 30.

cially interesting. The interviewer asked the Pope about his views on art, and what artists and writers he prefers. I was curious to see if some of the Pope's favorites might reveal something of his personality, and I was also curious to know if some of his favorites were also on my list of favorites.

The first writer that the Pope mentioned was Dostoyevsky. A few years ago, I took a course at St. John's University on the Russian novelist because I wanted to learn more about him. After the course was over, a seminarian and I met regularly to discuss the novel that many consider Dostoyevsky's masterpiece, *The Brothers Karamazov.* I wanted the student to study Dostoyevsky, but I also wanted the opportunity to re-read and discuss the masterpiece. Both the seminarian and I agreed that the novel is indeed a masterpiece and perhaps the greatest novel ever written, filled with marvelous insights.

In the interview, Father Spadaro reminds the Pope that in 2006 he said that the great artists know how to present the painful and tragic realities of life with beauty. I agree completely with Pope Francis' insight. Even a sad story can be beautiful. When I think of the filmmakers and novelists whose work I enjoy, I become very aware that often the stories they create are not very happy. For example, I think of the works of two of my favorite artists: the films of Ingmar Bergman and the novels of Graham Greene. A friend of mine does not like to see serious films. She says she goes to the movies "to be entertained." Of course, all moviegoers want to be entertained, but there are various ways to be entertained. Some of us find some serious films more entertaining than comedies that are poorly done and may even be dumb.

In responding to Father Spadaro, Pope Francis said the following:

> *"I have really loved a diverse array of authors. I love very much Dostoyevsky . . . I have read* The Betrothed, *by Alessandro Manzoni, three times, and I have it now on my table because I want to read it again. Manzoni gave me so much. When I was a child, my grandmother taught me by heart the beginning of* The Betrothed.*"* [12]

On the topic of films, Francis said the following:

> *"We should also talk about the cinema.* La Strada, *by Fellini, is the movie that perhaps I loved the most. I identify with the movie, in which there is an implicit reference to St. Francis. I also believe that I watched all of the Italian movies with Anna Magnani and Aldo Fabrizi when I was between 10 and 12 years old. Another film that I loved is* Rome, Open City. *I owe my film culture especially to my parents who used to take us to the movies quite often."* [13]

I think that if I had to guess before reading the interview what films were special to the Pope, I might have said Italian neo-realist films such as *La Strada* and *Rome, Open City*. The vision of the human mystery in *La Strada* is beautiful. The vision of the priesthood in *Rome, Open City* is marvelous and inspiring—something that every seminarian should see.

From the time that Pope Francis was elected, there

---

[12] Ibid., p. 32.
[13] Ibid., p. 34.

has been considerable speculation about what having a Jesuit as Pope will mean for the Church. I went to Xavier High School, a Jesuit high school located on West 16th Street in Manhattan. I imagine all the Jesuits who taught me, in fact all the Jesuits who were there almost sixty years ago, are now in heaven. However, I like to imagine how excited they would have been to have a Jesuit become Pope. Francis has emphasized St. Ignatius' notion of discernment. Rereading the interview has helped me to appreciate discernment in a new way. It now seems obvious to me that everyone, not only priests and religious, should engage in discernment especially when they are involved in making an important decision, a decision that will have serious ramifications in their lives. Francis hopes discernment will help us "to hear the things of God from God's 'point of view.' " [14]

There are all sorts of realities that can make seeing things from God's "point of view" very difficult. Our sinfulness, especially our pride, and the secular nature of our surroundings present obstacles to seeing things from God's "point of view." How we live will greatly enhance or hinder our being in tune with God's "point of view." Do I really want to "hear the things of God from God's point of view" or are my deepest desires coming from a selfish point of view in which I place myself, consciously or unconsciously, above God? In every sin, we place ourselves above God. Has my sinfulness not only made me deaf to hearing God's point of view but also moved me to replace God's point of view with my own point of view?

---

[14] Ibid., p. 17.

In addition to having someone with whom I can regularly discuss my relationship with God, usually called a spiritual director, I have discovered or rediscovered in recent years how being silent in God's presence can help us to see in new ways. If we allow ourselves to be totally honest before God and welcome God's loving presence, I think we will find that God "speaks" to us. We will "see" in a new way and have a sense of God's presence in a new way—a way that makes God's presence seem more real.

In the interview, the Holy Father, in commenting on the virtue of hope said, "God is all promise." [15] The theological virtue of hope is rooted in reality. Actually, it is rooted in God's presence in our lives. Hope does not disappoint because God does not disappoint. Hope does not assure us that everything we try to accomplish, even what we try to accomplish for God, will work out exactly the way we wish. It does guarantee that we are in the hands of God and that, ultimately, we cannot lose because God cannot lose. God uses our mistakes for good. In fact, even our sins are used by God and are woven into His providential plans. We are never alone. No decision we make, no choice we make takes place apart from the presence of a loving God. This should give us confidence and enable us to trust. God's love for us frees us to hope. There is a direction to history. Our earthly lives are meaningful, and we should never succumb to the temptation to think that we lack purpose, that we are insignificant, and that our lives have no importance. The astounding truth, which at times we may find difficult to believe, is that each of us has an

---

[15] Ibid., p. 32.

indispensable role in God's plan, that each of us is irre-
placeable. There is no such reality as an unimportant
person. I believe that each of us is called to be a gift-
giver and that makes us like God, Who is Gift-Giver.
My gift of myself is indispensable, and every person —
the rich and the poor, the geniuses and the mentally
challenged, the famous and the relatively unknown —
can make that statement. To be called to be a gift-giver
to others is one of the most profound truths about us. In
God's plan, each one of us is indispensable. No wonder
Pope Francis calls us to be people of hope.

Discussion Questions

1. What, if anything, do you think was new in the Pope's famous interview?

2. What did you find most interesting in the Pope's interview?

3. What does Pope Francis mean by "thinking with the Church"?

4. Is Pope Francis correct in saying that God is part of everyone's life? Can you think of anyone, past or present, who would be an exception?

5. What does Pope Francis think is an irreversible insight of Vatican II?

6. What do you think of the emphasis that Francis gave to the arts? Has any work of art had a profound influence on you?

7. How do you interpret the Pope's statement "God is all promise"?

Chapter Two

Apostolic Exhortation: "The Joy of the Gospel"

There are many insights in Francis' Apostolic Exhortation, "The Joy of the Gospel." Some of the insights are brilliant, several are beautiful, and many are inspiring.

Living as Graced Images of God

Reflecting on all the topics that Pope Francis writes about in the Exhortation I found Francis' insights into culture especially relevant. In trying to understand how important a culture is to help people grow in their faith or, unfortunately, how a culture can make it so difficult for people to believe and live as Christians, I find an idea that philosophers use helpful. The idea is expressed in the word "co-existence." It means that on every level of being human we co-exist with other persons.

Obviously, we co-exist with our parents and our siblings. I think it is just about impossible to overemphasize how much our parents and brothers and sisters influence us. Sigmund Freud, I have been told, thought

that between the ages of three and six our basic per-
sonalities are established for life. By the time we are six
years of age it's all over! I do not believe that, but I do
believe that when we are infants we are extremely
impressionable and so parents and siblings have a serious obligation to pass on good values. In schools, we are
dependent on teachers for knowledge. Throughout our
lives, and especially when we are young, we are deeply
affected emotionally by others. Of course, for better or
worse, the media can have a tremendous impact on us.
Pope Francis wrote the following about culture:

> *"The People of God is incarnate in the peoples of
> the earth, each of which has its own culture. The
> concept of culture is valuable for grasping the vari-
> ous expressions of the Christian life present in
> God's people. It has to do with the lifestyle of a given
> society, the specific way in which its members relate
> to one another, to other creatures and to God. Un-
> derstood in this way, culture embraces the totality
> of a people's life. Each people in the course of its his-
> tory develops its culture with legitimate autonomy.
> This is due to the fact that the human person, 'by
> nature stands completely in need of life in society'
> and always exists in reference to society, finding
> there a concrete way of relating to reality. The
> human person is always situated in culture: 'nature
> and culture are intimately linked.' Grace supposes
> culture, and God's gift becomes flesh in the culture
> of those who receive it."* [16]

If it is true that to live in intimate union with God,
so intimate that we share in God's intimate life of

---

[16] Pope Francis, Apostolic Exhortation of the Holy Father, *The Joy of the Gospel*,
(Boston: Pauline Book and Media, 2013), pp. 80-81, #15.

unlimited love, then the sharing ought to become visible at least occasionally in a culture. Of course, that sharing in God's life accounts for all the wonderful actions that people perform such as being merciful and forgiving, being unselfish, being concerned about those less fortunate and countless other good actions. But sharing God's life ought to inspire people to become educated so that they might help others and even be able to contribute to a culture's art, film, theater, music and literature. I am not suggesting that sharing God's life makes you a talented writer or musician or skilled in any other art form but I am suggesting that if God is pure self-gift and we share in God's life then we ought to try in any way we can to create a culture that helps people live as images of God.

For most of the years that I have been a priest, I have been involved in education. Partly because of my interests and partly, I hope, because of Providence, I have tried to interest seminarians, university students, and parishioners in literature and films that in one way or another reveal the mystery of God. I have no illusions about how successful my efforts have been, but even if only very few have been influenced by my apostolate, I will continue to try because I think it is what I should be doing as a university professor. I have a feeling Pope Francis would agree with me.

Attraction, not Proselytizing

There has been a great deal of talk in recent years about the new evangelization. Much that I have read or heard about it makes a great deal of sense to me but I find that some people do not have a clear idea about what it means to be an evangelizer. In "The Joy of the Gospel," Pope Francis makes some clear statements concerning evangelization. One of his statements about sharing joy should be emblazoned on the minds of those who try to get involved in the new evangelization. Francis points out that the new evangelization is a summons to all. He states that it is carried out in three principal settings. The first one he calls "ordinary pastoral ministry." The Holy Father includes within this activity those who, animated by the Holy Spirit, regularly take part in worship. He also includes in this setting those who sincerely believe and express their faith in various ways but do not take part in the Eucharist. A second area that Francis mentions includes those who are baptized but do not show in their lives the demands of Baptism. This would include people who do not have a meaningful relationship with the Church. My impression, and this may be due to my limited experience, is that the number in this group is increasing. Concerning the third setting, Pope Francis writes the following:

> *"Lastly, we cannot forget that evangelization is first and foremost about preaching the Gospel to* those who do not know Jesus Christ or who have always rejected him. *Many of them are quietly seeking God, led by a yearning to see his face, even in countries of ancient Christian tradition. All of them have a right to receive the Gospel. Christians have the duty to proclaim the Gospel without excluding anyone. Instead of seeming to impose new obligations, they should appear as people who wish to share their joy, who point to a horizon of*

beauty, and who invite others to a delicious banquet. It is not by proselytizing that the Church grows, but 'by attraction.' " [17]

Pope Francis is calling attention to something very important when he says that evangelizers should not seem to impose new obligations but rather should appear as joyful people who want to share their joy. I think the idea that evangelizers should be people who point to a horizon of beauty is marvelous. Perhaps when people are encouraged to give good example they might think "What a trite idea. Is that all we have to do? Is not there something more important that we can do?" I once thought that way but I have changed my mind. I wonder if there is anything more important than giving good example. Every person I know who has experienced a religious conversion has been moved toward that conversion through some believer who made a deep impression or whose life and faith were so attractive that they challenged someone to self-reflection that eventually led to a religious conversion. I am not sure I ever met anyone who was converted because of an idea. It seems to be true that most people are most influenced by other people.

That the lives of evangelizers can point to a horizon of beauty is a wonderful image. The beauty of God and the beauty of God's involvement with people ought to shine forth in the lives of evangelizers. No one is inviting someone to embrace an interesting set of ideas. Evangelizers are bearing witness to a relationship they have with God and are inviting others to encounter Christ. That invitation comes more through the lives of

---

[17] Ibid., p. 11., #14.

evangelizers than through their words. The Pope's insistence that the Church grows through attraction challenges all of us.

About a year ago, I received a compliment from a student at St. John's, though I am sure the student, who was not a Catholic, did not realize he was complimenting me. I am also not sure I deserved the compliment. The student has a relative who is Christian but perhaps a Christian who finds being a Christian more of a burden than a joy. The student must have been describing me to his relative, and she told him to ask me a question, which he did. The question was "How come you are always so happy?" For a few seconds I was stunned. I am a happy person, but I guess I was surprised that the student was struck by this. I eventually said something like, "If you believed what I believe you would be happy too. I believe I am unconditionally loved by God. Why shouldn't I be happy?" After the meeting with that student was over, I wondered if I had ever received a more wonderful compliment from a student.

Pope Francis' Optimism

I have been thinking about why I find Francis' writing so inspiring. Given his popularity, my guess is that I am not the only one who finds his insights inspiring. Certainly, the Holy Father's style of writing appeals to me. His compassion and stress on God's mercy also appeals to me. I find his insights very provocative and I am beginning to think that what makes Francis' writing so attractive is his holiness. Somehow, his goodness and closeness to God come through in what Francis writes. Reflecting on the goodness of people, Francis writes the following:

> *"To understand this reality we need to approach it with the gaze of the Good Shepherd, who seeks not to judge but to love. Only from the affective connaturality born of love can we appreciate the theological life present in the piety of Christian peoples, especially among the poor. I think of the steadfast faith of those mothers tending their sick children who, though perhaps barely familiar with the articles of the creed, cling to a rosary; or of all the hope poured into a candle lighted in a humble home with a prayer for help from Mary, or in the gaze of tender love directed to Christ crucified. No one who loves God's holy people will view these actions as the expression of a purely human search for the divine. They are the manifestation of a theological life nourished by the working of the Holy Spirit who has been poured into our hearts."* [18]

I do not know how many times I have read the above quotation but every time I read it I am moved by the Pope's love of people, and his profound understanding of them. Francis is a very wise man.

What does the Pope mean by "connaturality"? There can be a special type of familiarity produced by frequent experience. Possibly this might be expressed as a knowledge due to a loving familiarity with some reality. One example would be a farmer who has a connatural knowledge of the weather. His knowledge has been drawn not from books but from his experience of farming outdoors, working in various temperatures in snow,

---

[18] Ibid., pp. 88-89, #125.

rain, and sun. The notion of connaturality suggests that the farmer's experience goes beyond that of a person who makes weather forecasts on television. The farmer knows in a special way and that is what the word "connaturality" is an attempt at expressing. Affective connaturality born of love stresses that the knowledge comes through loving and identifying in some way with the reality known. Francis is suggesting that love of God and familiarity with God's presence in our lives will dispose us toward the piety of Christian people and deter us from reducing some devotions to nothing but emotional experiences.

As I am writing this, an image of my mother comes to me. My mother knew little theology and was not interested in knowing more. Commenting on my weekly columns and on some books that I had written, she would say something like, "Why are you writing all these columns and books? No one knows what you are talking about!" But every morning that I was home, for as far back as I can remember, my mother sat in her favorite chair in our living room and with the rosary in her hands said her daily prayers. This was a daily ritual right up to her death. Francis would have admired that kind of devotion.

Reading Francis' remarks about "theological life nourished by the working of the Holy Spirit," I am upset that the media stresses all the bad events that are happening in the world and neglects so many good events and actions that are happening. A constant diet of bad news has to have an effect on us. When we remind ourselves of the countless good actions that are being performed around the world but that receive little if any attention in the media, our perspective on the world can change. The Holy Spirit is operative everywhere! I believe that the Holy Spirit is influencing people who profess their faith in the Spirit's presence in their lives. However, I also believe that the Holy Spirit is active in the lives of many who do not believe in the Spirit and may never even have heard of the Holy Spirit. I think Pope Francis believes that too.

Discussion Questions

1. Do you think our culture is helping you as a Christian?

2. Do you agree with the Pope's emphasis on joy?

3. Should Pope Francis, and all of us, be optimistic in the contemporary world?

4. Do you think that a "constant diet of bad news" has a negative effect on you?

Chapter Three

Insights from Personalism

D ivisions in categorizing periods in the History of Philosophy are rarely clear-cut. Occasionally a thinker is sufficiently different from predecessors that his thought clearly heralds a new way of thinking. Rene Descartes (1596-1650) is clearly such a thinker. His embrace of science and mathematics as the best ways of knowing because of their clarity, earns him the title "the Father of Modern Philosophy," and identifies his philosophy as a break with the previous period of medieval philosophy and very different from what is usually characterized as contemporary philosophy.

Personalism is a twentieth and twenty-first century philosophy. Plato, Aristotle, and Thomas Aquinas were great thinkers, perhaps the greatest in the history of philosophy, but though they pointed in various ways to the dignity of the human person, they were not personalists.

Four thinkers who deserve the title "personalists," and whose thinking has greatly influenced my own, are Martin Buber (1878-1965), Gabriel Marcel (1889-1973), Emmanuel Mounier (1905-1950), and W. Norris Clarke, S.J. (1915-2008). I have no idea how much Francis has read any of these four thinkers, but a strong personalistic emphasis is evident in the Holy Father's thought. Whether the influence of personalism is due to Francis' direct reading of these thinkers, or whether the influence of their type of thinking was absorbed by the Holy Father indirectly, is a project for historians of thought to study. For our purposes, a less scholarly approach is sufficient. My approach is to use insights from personalism to illuminate the vision of person that is, at least implicitly, present in everything that Pope Francis says or writes.

In describing personalism, Emmanuel Mounier writes:

> "...one may openly live the experiment of personal life, hoping to convert to it a number of others who still live like trees, like animals or like machines. Bergson called for 'the appeal of the hero or the saint.' But these words must not deceive us: the personal appeal may spring from the humblest levels of human life. "This brings us to the central paradox of personal existence. The personal is the mode of existence proper to man. Nevertheless, it has ceaselessly to be attained: consciousness itself can but gradually disengage itself from the mineral, the plant and the animal which weigh it down. "The history of the person, therefore, runs parallel with that of personalism. It will not unfold itself on the plane of consciousness alone, but throughout the length and breadth of the human struggle to humanize humanity." [19]

We are confronted with the perennial question:

---

[19] Emmanuel Mounier, *Personalism*, (Translated by Philip Mairet. Notre Dame, Indiana: University of Notre Dame Press, 1952), p. xix.

"Which came first, the egg or the chicken?" Did elements of personalism lead to the freeing of the slaves, to women's right to vote, to the civil rights movement, to the peace movement, to the great emphasis on person in the documents of Vatican II, or did those events lead to the development and growth of personalism? Probably there is an ongoing interaction between a personalistic vision and action. In this chapter, I will sketch a few central ideas in the personalism of Buber, Marcel, Mounier, and Clarke to provide a background to the personalism that permeates Francis' thought.

Buber is famous for his depiction of what he calls I-Thou and I-It relationships. [20] In an I-It relationship, one person treats the other as an object, as someone to be used. If I approach a person as an "it," and I ask "Who are you?" I mean, "What can you do for me? How can I use you? What function can you perform in my life?"

The I-It relationship is dramatically different from the I-Thou relationship. In an I-Thou relationship, I meet the other at the center of his or her being and that is how the other meets me. Buber claimed that there were five characteristics to every I-Thou. Such a relationship is ineffable, intense, direct, mutual and involves a special presence. The I-Thou is ineffable. No one, not even Buber, can understand it completely. It is intense. It can actually change lives. It is direct in that it focuses on the center of the person, beyond all physical characteristics. It is mutual. It takes two. No one can force an I-Thou relationship to happen. A person

---

[20] Martin Buber, *I and Thou*, (New Translation by Walter Kaufman, New York: Charles Soulner's Sens, 1970), p. 185.

can be ready and open for such a relationship but the other must respond. The special presence in an I-Thou relationship is that each person is present *for the other*.

Especially important in Buber's vision is that God is present in each I-Thou relationship. God is the Thou behind every thou. This means that in every I-Thou relationship each person is also meeting God. So an atheist who has an I-thou relationship with his wife is also meeting God. Buber claimed that a person could have an I-Thou relationship with another human person, with God, and with an object of nature. The latter immediately brings to my mind Pope Francis' magnificent encyclical on the environment *Laudato Si*, but more about that later. Buber believed that when an I-Thou with God slipped into an I-It, it was no longer God to whom the person was relating. God is the Thou Who can never become an "It."

In the translation I am using, the word "You" is used for "Thou." Buber wrote the following:

> *"Three are the spheres in which the world of relation arises. The first: life with nature. Here the relation vibrates in the dark and remains below language. The creatures stir across from us, but they are unable to come to us, and the You we say to them sticks to the threshold of language. The second: life with men. Here the relation is manifest and enters language. We can give and receive the You. The third: life with spiritual beings. Here the relation is wrapped in a cloud but reveals itself, it lacks but creates language. We hear no You and yet feel addressed, we answer—creating, thinking, acting: with our being we speak the basic word, unable to say You with our mouth. But how can we incor-*

porate into the world of the basic word what lies outside language? In every sphere, through everything that becomes present to us, we gaze toward the train of the eternal You; in each we perceive a breath of it, in every You we address the eternal You, in every sphere according to its manner." [21]

Buber is eloquent on love.

"Love is a cosmic force. For those who stand in it and behold in it, men emerge from their entanglement in busy-ness, and the good and the evil, the clever and the foolish, the beautiful and the ugly, one after another become actual and a You for them, that is liberated, emerging into a unique confrontation. Exclusiveness comes into being miraculously again and again—and now one can act, help, heal, educate, raise, redeem. Love is a responsibility of an I for a You: in this consists what cannot consist in any feeling—the equality of all lovers, from the smallest to the greatest and from the blissfully secure whose life is circumscribed by the life of one beloved human being to him that is nailed his life long to the cross of the world, capable of what is immense and bold enough to risk it: to love man." [22]

Emmanuel Mounier's insights into the mystery of person are as beautiful and provocative as Buber's. Mounier writes:

"I am a person from my most elementary existence upward, and my embodied existence, far from de-personalizing me, is a factor essential to my personal status. My body is not one object among others, nor even the nearest object—for how then could

---
[21] Ibid., pp. 56-57.
[22] Ibid., pp. 66-67.

it be one with my experience as a subject? In fact the two experiences are not separate: I exist subjectively, I exist bodily *are one and the same experience. I cannot think without being and I cannot be without my body, which is my exposition—to myself, to the world, to everyone else. By its means alone can I escape from the solitude of a thinking that would only be thought about thought. By its refusal to leave me wholly transparent to myself, the body takes me constantly out of myself into the problems of the world and the struggles of mankind. By the solicitation of the senses it pushes me out into space, by growing old it acquaints me with duration, and by its death, it confronts me with eternity."* [23]

I find Mounier especially eloquent and challenging in his thoughts about love:

"Real love is creative of distinction; it is gratitude and a will towards another because he is other than oneself..."This communion of love, in liberating him who responds to it, also liberates and reassures him who offers it. Love is the surest certainty that man knows; the one irrefutable, existential cogito: I love, therefore I am, therefore being is, and life has value (is worth the pain of living).*

"Love does not reassure me simply as a state of being in which I find myself, for it gives me to someone else . . . it shakes me out of my self-assurance, my habits, my egocentric torpor: communication even when hostile, is the thing that most reveals me to myself." [24]

---

[23] Mounier, op. cit. p. 11.
[24] Ibid., p. 23.

Marcel's emphasis on the mystery of being is so strong that he suggested that when we talk about God, it is not God about Whom we are talking. Similar to Buber's insistence that if an I-Thou relationship with God slips into an I-It relationship, then it is no longer God to whom a person is relating, Marcel was wary that talk *about* God could reduce God to an object. Rather than speaking *about* God, Marcel believed that God should be spoken *to* in prayer. [25]

In his excellent book on Marcel, Seymour Cain writes:

> *"Religious worship for Marcel is the paradigmatic act of being-with, of ontological communion, of opening-up and adherence to being. It is only in worship that any intimate knowledge of the Absolute Thou may be obtained; indeed, worship may be viewed as the starting-point for any philosophy of transcendence, and there may be a close analogy between worship and metaphysical vision or contemplation, with a common source in 'wonder.'"* [26]

The special contribution of Jesuit priest-philosopher Clarke is indeed *special*. In wedding Thomism and Personalism, Clarke I believe made an original contribution to philosophy. Viewing the human person as dynamically oriented both intellectually and volitionally toward the Infinite, Clarke wrote:

> *"The human intellect, as capacity for being* (capax entis) *is naturally ordered, as to its ade-*

---

[25] Seymour Cain, *Gabriel Marcel*, (South Bend, Indiana: Regnery/Gateway, Inc., Book Publishers, 1979), p. 128.
[26] Ibid., p. 93.

quate object, to the whole of being as intelligible. Hence, it can ultimately be satisfied only by knowing directly the infinite source and fullness of all being, namely God (capax entis, ergo capax Dei*). So too the human will, the faculty tending towards being as good, is naturally ordered to the whole order of the good without restriction. Hence, it too cannot be ultimately satisfied by anything less than loving union with God as the infinite fullness of all goodness. Thus we are magnetized, so to speak, by our very nature toward the Infinite Good, which draws us in our very depths, at first spontaneously below the level of consciousness and freedom, but then slowly emerging into consciousness as we grow older—if we allow it—by the accumulation of experience and reflection upon it."* [27]

Clarke gives a succinct description of the deepening relationships to which a person is called.

"Let us explore more in detail this relational aspect of the human person, beginning from the bottom up. The initial relationality of the human person towards the outer world of nature and other persons is primarily receptive, in need of actualizing its latent potentialities from without. The human person as child first goes out towards the world as poor, as appealingly but insistently needy. The primary response partner is the mother, who meets the growing person's needs ideally with caring love. First she responds to the physical and basic needs, then slowly draws forth over the early years the active interpersonal response of the child as an I to herself as Thou, by her active relating to

---

[27] W. Norris Clarke, *Person and Being*, (Milwaukee: Marquette University Press, 1993), pp. 36-37.

the child precisely as a loving I to a unique, special, and beloved Thou, not just as a useful or interesting object or thing, or another instance of human nature. John Macmurray has beautifully described the process of personalization, of drawing out of latent potentiality the self-conscious awareness and active interpersonal response of the growing child-person, first by the mother or her surrogate, then by the father, the whole family, the neighborhood community, the school, etc." [28]

I cannot think of any part of the four philosophers' vision with which Pope Francis would disagree. The vision that these thinkers present, is the underlying vision present, either explicitly or implicitly, in just about everything Pope Francis says or writes. Of course, because the Holy Father's personalism is explicitly Trinitarian, the insights offered by thinkers such as Buber, Marcel, Mounier, and Clarke are taken to a new level, with new depth. The presence of the Holy Spirit opening people to the Risen Christ and enabling them to have an intimate relationship with the Incarnate God, in whose image all persons are created, is essential to what Francis proclaims.

---

[28] Ibid., pp. 72-73.

Discussion Questions

1. Judging from the writings by personalist philosophers quoted in Chapter 3, which philosopher
   appeals to you the most? Why?

2. What signs of personalism can you observe in the
   contemporary world?

3. What is an I-Thou relationship? Do you have any?
   Does anyone treat you like an "it"?

4. Is Father W. Norris Clarke's description of human
   knowing and loving correct?

Chapter Four

A Revolution of Love

Cardinal Walter Kaspar's *Pope Francis' Revolution of Tenderness and Love*, is an important book. An excellent theologian, Cardinal Kaspar knows Pope Francis' theological vision and Pope Francis' spirituality very well. In his first chapter, which he entitles "Pope of Surprises," Cardinal Kaspar, claiming that the election of Francis seemed to come at a providential moment, writes:

> *"The cases of abuse had unleashed a shock wave and caused serious damage, above all in the United Sates, Ireland, Belgium, and Germany. Additionally, there arose the impression of mental fatigue and exhaustion, a lack of confidence and enthusiasm. The church was increasingly occupied primarily with itself; it suffered and moaned about its situation or occasionally celebrated itself. Its prophetic power appeared extinguished and its missionary vitality appeared to languish. A world that had become secular and that was no longer communist, but rather consumerist and determined by the economy, appeared to make the church marginal. Booming Pentecostal churches and esotericism throughout the world threatened to*

outstrip it. A relentless downward spiral appeared to be in motion." [29]

How much can one man accomplish? Of course, I do not know the answer to that question but I would hesitate to think that Pope Francis could not accomplish a great deal. By changing attitudes and renewing hope, I think that he has accomplished a great deal. He has dramatically changed the atmosphere. Besides what he can accomplish in his own lifetime, who can tell what legacy he will leave, how much his initiatives will reap beneficial results for years to come?

I know that the Holy Father's profound concern about the poor has provoked my conscience and made me decide that I must become much more knowledgeable about the Church's social teaching. I want to know it sufficiently well that I can see how it should influence my own efforts at living the Christian life, my efforts teaching at St. John's and my efforts to preach at Eucharistic celebrations.

I want to see more clearly and deeply how the Church's social teaching is not just an addendum to the faith, or an interesting philosophical view about society, but is intimately related to Jesus' death and resurrection and to our salvation and redemption.

I have become aware that I have been reacting toward this Pope in a way that I have never reacted to any other Pope. Of course, like any Catholic, and especially as a Catholic priest, I have always accepted the teaching of any Pope and have tried to promote that

---

[29] Walter Kaspar, *Pope Francis' Revolution of Tenderness and Love: Theological and Pastoral Perspectives*, (Translated by William Madges. New Jersey: Paulist Press, 2015), p. 2.

teaching in any way that I could. So far, I do not think that Pope Francis has changed any Church teaching but he has changed the atmosphere in the Church and the image of the Church and the papacy outside of the Church. This is no small accomplishment. He has attracted the interest of both Catholics and others and won the affection of many, myself included.

Reflecting on my own enthusiastic reaction to Pope Francis, I have had difficulty clearly understanding what is different about it in relation to my reaction to other Popes. As far back as Pius XII, I have admired every man who led the Catholic Church. Two of them are canonized saints. So what is different about my own reaction to this Holy Father? Somehow, I have experienced the comments of Pope Francis as personally directed to me. I do not mean that the Holy Father is not reaching many, but I do mean that his leadership and commitment to the Gospel inspires me just about every time I read or hear about some statement he has made.

Early in his book, Cardinal Kaspar notes that he is not going to be dealing with biographical details, anecdotes and stories, and certainly not with gossip about the private details dealing with what really or supposedly is happening behind the Vatican walls. Indicating what he is trying to do in his small volume, Cardinal Kaspar writes the following:

> *"In the following, the attempt will be made to approach the Francis phenomenon theologically and to illuminate somewhat the theological background and the theological substance of his pontificate, and to make clear the new perspectives that are emerging. The positive as well as the critical*

*assessments are in danger of trivializing or treating
the pontificate in a banal manner. If some turn the
Pope into a kind of rock star, so others regard him
as a theological lightweight. Pope Francis is neither the one nor the other . . . The surprisingly new
features of this 'Pope of surprises' are not some
innovations, but rather the eternal newness of the
gospel, which is always the same and yet, over and
over again, is surprisingly new and always relevant in a new way."* [30]

I think that what drew me to Cardinal Kaspar's book
was the opportunity to understand better what is different in Pope Francis' theology and what is different in
his approach to problems. Kaspar points out that Pope
Francis starts not with doctrine or theology but with
the concrete situation. Then he tries to discern what in
God's revelation and in the Church's teaching might
apply and illuminate the concrete situation. Kaspar
suggests that the Holy Father, after studying a situation, asks himself "What does God want of me in this
situation?" Kaspar points out that the great Jesuit theologian Karl Rahner (1904-1984) spoke of an existential
knowledge, meaning the knowledge of the concrete will
of God that is available to the individual in a given situation. Of course, this does not mean that Francis will
change God's Revelation or change the Church's teaching. It means that his starting point is different from
his papal predecessors.

I very much like Rahner's notion of existential
knowledge. It seems to me that this is the type of
knowledge that each and every one of us should strive

---

[30] Ibid., pp. 7, 8.

for in our lives. At this moment in my life, what is God asking of me? What does God want from me at this time in my life? Where is God leading me? God's love and providential will accompany us every second of our lives. I hope I never forget that. To believe that God is lovingly present every moment should both console and challenge us. That belief can color everything we do. We are never alone.

Cardinal Kaspar points out that following the lead of Pope St. John XXIII, the bishops at the Second Vatican Council started with the concrete situation in the world as they tried to read the "signs of the times." It is quite possible that Pope Francis, like the Council, will lead the Church to a new birth that will inspire and instruct not only Catholics, but also all persons of good will. That is one of the hopes I have as I observe Pope Francis' leadership.

In the first few months of his pontificate, Pope Francis was depicted, at least in some reports, as though he was entirely different from the Popes who had preceded him. The impression was that there was little connection between Francis and his predecessors. Of course, this was a very wrong impression. Cardinal Walter Kaspar, noting the different backgrounds of Pope Benedict and Pope Francis, writes the following:

> *"The difference between Pope Benedict and Pope Francis thus goes back far, but it does not concern theological truth. Rather, it concerns theological method and its concomitant emphases, as well as Pope Francis' style, which is less didactic and more kerygmatic. With reference to the old as well as the more recent history of the papacy, such differences are nothing new, but rather are an expression of*

Catholic unity in diversity, as well as a sign of a not defunct but living tradition that is guided by God's Spirit. The entire history of the papacy is full of such unity in diversity and difference." [31]

Cardinal Kaspar suggests that the method developed by the founder of the Young Christian Workers, Cardinal Joseph Cardijn (1881-1967), had a strong influence on Pope Francis before he became Pope. The method of the Young Christian Workers was observe, judge, act. When I read this in Kaspar's book, many wonderful memories came back to me. When I was a young parish priest in the early 1960s, I was the chaplain for four Catholic Action movements: The Young Christian Workers, the Young Christian Students (college level), the Young Christian Students (high school level) and the Christian Family Movement. All these movements used the method developed by Cardinal Cardijn: observe, judge, act.

I would meet regularly with members of these Catholic Action groups and they would focus in on some problem, usually in the parish, observe the situation, make a judgment about what could be done about the problem and then take some action to try to correct the problem. These meetings were very encouraging and even inspiring for me. The enthusiasm and commitment of the people involved encouraged me to be enthusiastic and committed. The people involved in the Catholic Action groups took their faith seriously and wanted to bear witness to Christ in their daily lives. I suspect that I received much more from the members of these groups than they received from me. Looking back

[31] Ibid., p. 12.

on those early days of my priestly ministry, I marvel at the impact that those Catholic Action groups had on me. I suspect that Pope Francis is using the method of observe, judge, act as he leads the Church.

Cardinal Kaspar is very good on just what the Church means by tradition, the tradition that Pope Francis is handing on in his teaching. Cardinal Kaspar writes the following:

> *"Tradition is the content of the apostolic inheritance that is binding for all times, as well as realized ever anew in the Holy Spirit. In this sense, tradition is understood by the Second Vatican Council as a living tradition, in which, with the aid of the Holy Spirit, there is progress and growth in the understanding of the apostolic faith that has been handed on once and for all....*
>
> *"...Pope Francis wants to clear away many of the accumulated ashes in order to bring to light anew the fiery nucleus of the gospel. If one wants to speak of a revolution, then it is not a revolution in the sense of a violent overthrow, but rather, as Francis says, the fervent revolution of tender love, upon whose transforming power from within he relies."* [32]

The expression "revolution of tender love" is beautiful and provocative. What does it suggest? It suggests that we cannot force people to believe nor should we want to force faith on people. Faith has to be a free act. Does that mean we do nothing? Of course not. The "revolution of tender love" suggests that we bear witness with our lives. If our lives bear witness to Christ, if it is obvious that Christ is the center of our lives, we will be

---

[32] Ibid., p. 13.

tapping into divine power. The expression "revolution of tender love" suggests that we believe in the power of love, indeed that we believe that love is the most powerful force in the universe. Through the power of love, even death has been conquered in Jesus' resurrection. I once thought that bearing witness with our lives was not doing very much. Now I believe there is nothing more important that we can do. Lives of committed love are powerful signs that attract.

What has made Cardinal Walter Kaspar especially interesting to me is that he seems to know the Holy Father's theology and spiritual approach to problems very well. Reading the book, I have had the impression that I am gaining an inside look into how Francis thinks and how he looks at problems. For me this makes Cardinal Kaspar's small volume something special.

One of the great influences on Pope Francis' thinking was the theologian Lucio Gera (1924-2012). Kaspar points out that when he was Archbishop Bergoglio, Francis arranged to have Gera interred in the episcopal crypt of the Buenos Aires Cathedral in order to honor Gera as the father of Argentine theology. Cardinal Kaspar writes the following:

> *"Lucio Gera, together with Gustavo Gutierrez, who is regarded as the father of liberation theology, and others took part in the conference in Petropolis in 1964 that had been convened by the Latin American Episcopal Conference (CELAM). It is regarded as the hour in which liberation theology was born. At this conference, Lucio Gera gave a paper on the theme 'The Meaning of the Christian Message in the Context of Poverty and Oppression.'*

This theme has become foundational for all forms of liberation theology. They all operate according to the method of see, judge, act." [33]

When I first began teaching philosophy at St. John's University thirty years ago, there was a course in the theology department on liberation theology. At that time, some students misunderstood liberation theology. Because the course dealt with social conditions, some students thought it was a sociology course rather than a theology course. Their judgment about the course was erroneous: it was a theology course not a sociology course. I think that in some people's minds liberation theology involves the embracing of Marxism. It does not. Marx was an atheist. A Catholic theology cannot be based on atheism. Liberation theology tries to look at Christian Revelation from the perspective of the poor in order to see what light Christian revelation can shed on poverty. Cardinal Kaspar describes Argentine theology as a theology of the people and of culture. It seems that in his pontificate Francis has been using the method of see, judge, and act. As Cardinal Kaspar points out, Pope Francis starts not with an idea but with reality.

Cardinal Kaspar indicates that Francis was also influenced by the great German theologian, Romano Guardini. I was delighted to learn this. Guardini was a very popular writer among seminarians when I was a student in the major seminary in the 50s. I have probably read seven or eight of his books. I recall that a common practice was for seminarians to pass on to friends the books that they had read and thought were special.

[33] Ibid., p. 21.

Guardini was one of the most popular authors. I suspect that his book, *The Lord*, is considered a spiritual classic.

Cardinal Kaspar offers the following summary statement of Francis' theology:

> *"...he wants to shed light on the situation of the church and of Christians in the contemporary world from the perspective of the gospel. In so doing, Christian faith is not an ideology that tends to explain everything; it is not to be compared with a floodlight that illuminates the entire path of our life. Rather, it is like a lantern that shines for us on the path of life as far as we ourselves are advancing. It is a forever surprising, never exhaustible message of joy."* [34]

What especially appeals to me in Francis' outlook on reality under the light of the Gospel, is his emphasis on joy. It is no accident that he called his magnificent Apostolic Exhortation "The Joy of the Gospel." Francis does not present the Christian life as a life that is weighed down with a great burden. Rather he presents it, even though Christian commitment involves sacrifices, at times great sacrifices, as a life that should lead to profound joy. Ultimately living as a Christian should lead to profound joy, a joy that can co-exist with sacrifices, even with crosses and suffering. Joy should be the "bottom line," the ultimate and deepest reaction to the Gospel. I love Francis' emphasis on joy.

Noting that the reading of Sacred Scripture and reflecting on it is essential for Pope Francis, Cardinal Kaspar makes the important point that for Pope

---

[34] Ibid., p. 23-24.

Francis the Gospel does not mean a book or the four books that we call the four Gospels. Kaspar comments that originally the word "gospel" meant a message, the delivery of a good and liberating message, one that changes the situation. The "gospel" means a message that confronts the listener with a new situation and calls for him or her to make a decision. Cardinal Kaspar writes:

> *"In the Old Testament, good news is the message of the imminent return of the people Israel from Babylonian captivity; in the New Testament, it is Jesus' own message of the coming of God's kingdom and the message of Jesus the Christ, of his death and his resurrection as the exalted Lord who is effectively present in the church and in the world through his Spirit; it is the message of hope for his final coming and of the dawn and gift of new life. So what matters to Francis is the good news of God, which is proclaimed, believed, celebrated, and lived in a spiritual way in the church. For him it is a gospel of joy in the sense of a holistic fulfillment of life that God alone, who is all in all, can give."* [35]

The word from Cardinal Kaspar's description of Gospel as message in the Old Testament and in the New Testament that leaps out at me is "holistic." My dictionary has the following description of "holistic": "concerned with, or dealing with integrated systems rather than with their parts." The message from God is an integrated message, a message that covers every aspect of our lives. It is a message that should cause us to have a profound joy. This should be a joy that can be

---

[35] Ibid., p. 24.

retained, celebrated, and deepened even in the presence of suffering and crosses. Francis is calling our attention to the entire Christian message and to its liberating power. He is also trying to help us see how the message can illuminate our experience. There is no aspect of life that cannot be illuminated by the Christian Gospel. In his pontificate, Pope Francis has made very clear his concern for the poor and his zeal in teaching the Church's doctrine of social justice. Cardinal Kaspar points out that though the Holy Father is deeply concerned about social justice, the contemporary problem to which the joy of the Gospel speaks goes much deeper than social injustice. Kaspar identifies the problem in the following way:

> *"It concerns the lack of joy and the lack of spirit, the inner emptiness and the isolation of human persons closed up in themselves and the loneliness of hearts turned in on themselves. . . . Ultimately, his talk about the lack of joy and energy traces back to what, from the early desert fathers up to Thomas Aquinas, is regarded as the basic sin and original temptation of human beings: the* acedia, *the indolence of the heart, the gravitational pull dragging one down, the sluggishness, the weariness in spiritual matters that leads to the unhappiness of this world."* [36]

Indicating that Pope Francis is not alone in his analysis of contemporary culture, Cardinal Kaspar points out that similar analyses have been made by thinkers such as Soren Kierkegaard, the father of existentialism, and Romano Guardini. The cardinal also

---

[36] Ibid., p. 25-26.

mentions Martin Heidegger's insights into anxiety as our basic disposition and Jean Paul Sartre's focus on the ennui of the contemporary human person. I agree completely with the Holy Father's analysis of contemporary society and of the ennui that many are experiencing. Each person who professes belief in the Gospel has the responsibility to be a witness to what he or she believes. This does not mean we have to proselytize or preach. More important than preaching with words will be our experience of Christian joy that will speak to others much more than any words we utter. I think our task is to allow the Gospel to cause a profound joy in our lives. That joy may be the best message we can give.

As I have mentioned, Cardinal Kaspar points out that for Francis the Gospel does not mean a written document, but the message of Jesus of the coming of God's kingdom, a message of His death and resurrection and a message of hope for His final coming. Cardinal Kaspar writes:

> *"In Thomas Aquinas'* Summa Theologiae *we find an article of surprising originality concerning the new law of the gospel, to which Pope Francis refers explicitly in* Evangelii Gaudium *(EG37, 43). In this article, Thomas explains that the Gospel is not a written law or code of doctrines and commandments, but rather is the inner gift of the Holy Spirit, which is given to us in faith and is active in love. Writings and regulations belong only secondarily to the gospel; they are supposed to direct us to the gift of grace or to make it effective. However, they have no independent grace-mediating signifi-*

cance, and that means they have no independent significance for justification." [37]

I think put simply that means that the written texts are to lead us more deeply into union with the Holy Spirit. The presence of the Spirit within us is not for the sake of the texts but rather the written texts are to nourish us, to lead us into a more intimate relationship with God. Using traditional Catholic theological language, we could say the texts are to help us grow in sanctifying grace. Kaspar explains that Pope Francis does not want to cause a revolution in faith and morals but rather to interpret faith and morals from the perspective of the Gospel. Noting that Francis is proclaiming the Gospel, Kaspar emphasizes that Francis does not teach in some abstract, didactic manner but rather in a simple dialogical manner that speaks to people. Even early in his pontificate I think it was obvious that Pope Francis gets through to people. Kasper stresses that Pope Francis wants people to live joyfully a life of faith.

The fifth chapter of Cardinal Kaspar's book is entitled "Mercy—The Key Word of His Pontificate," and in that chapter, Cardinal Kaspar who has written an absolutely terrific book on mercy, *Mercy: The Essence of the Gospel and the Key to Christian Life*, persuasively argues that for Francis mercy stands at the center of the Gospel. I find it interesting that on the cover of Kaspar's book on mercy is the following statement from the Holy Father: "This book has done me much good."

---

[37] Ibid., p. 29.

Commenting on God's mercy, Kaspar writes:

"One could say that as God's fidelity to himself, mercy is simultaneously God's fidelity to his covenant and is his steadfast forbearance with human beings. In his mercy, God leaves no one in the lurch. Divine mercy gives everyone a new chance and grants everyone a new beginning, if he or she is eager for conversion and asks for it. . . . Let it, however, be understood: mercy justifies the sinner, not the sin." [38]

If that is not good news, I do not know what is!

Kaspar makes the important point that the Church does not create truth out of its own power or resources. Rather the Church is able to teach truth because she listens to the word of God, especially in the Eucharist. Kaspar quotes from the Holy Father's *The Joy of the Gospel*:

"All evangelization is based on that word, listened to, meditated upon, lived, celebrated and witnessed to . . . The church does not evangelize unless she constantly lets herself be evangelized. It is indispensable that the word of God be ever more fully at the heart of every ecclesial activity. God's word, listened to and celebrated, above all in the Eucharist, nourishes and inwardly strengthens Christians, enabling them to offer an authentic witness to the Gospel in daily life. . . . The preaching of the word, living and effective, prepares for the reception of the sacrament, and in the sacrament that word attains its maximum efficacy." [39]

---

[38] Ibid., pp. 32-33.
[39] Ibid., p. 42.

I think that the Pope's insistence that the Church let herself be evangelized is extremely important. While perfect in its head, the Risen Christ, the Church is not perfect in its members. Renewal in faith should be taking place not just when there is an ecumenical council but daily in the life of the Church, daily in the life of each of us. From the Holy Father to the most recent convert, to be part of the people of God is to be on a journey of faith.

Cardinal Kaspar suggests that a key word to describe Francis' vision of the Church is mission. Francis does not only see the Church as preserving Christ's truth but sees the Church as a missionary community. Kaspar stresses that Francis does not see the Church as growing through proselytizing but rather through attraction. For me this is an extremely important point. If we Christians really believe what we claim to believe, our faith should color all our activities, indeed it should color our entire life. Our faith and joy will be genuine and will attract people. Are not Francis' faith and joy appealing to people? Are not his faith and joy attractive? How else can we explain the impact that this man has had, not only on Catholics, but also on people of other faiths and on people who claim they have no faith at all? The impact that Francis has already had is nothing short of amazing. What a phenomenon! Almost everyone is excited about this Pope and seems to be inspired by Francis.

Noting that Francis emphasizes the doctrine of the People of God, Cardinal Kaspar writes the following:

> *"Francis speaks of a mysticism of coexistence and encounter, of embracing and supporting one*

another, of participating in a caravan of solidarity, in sacred pilgrimage (EG 87)...he speaks of a mystical and contemplative fraternity, 'which knows how to see the sacred grandeur of our neighbor, of finding God in every human being' (EG 92)." [40]

I confess that I find the "mysticism of coexistence and encounter" both absolutely beautiful and challenging. What coexistence means is that on every level of being human we depend on and are influenced by others. That this coexisting has a mystical dimension means that the Holy Spirit is present in every human encounter and in every human relationship. The word "encounter" has personalism written all over it. By a "mystical and contemplative fraternity," I think Francis is pointing out that the Holy Spirit enables us to see the deepest truth about other persons, namely that each person is a temple of the Holy Spirit. If we allowed that truth to guide our lives, there really would be a revolution of tenderness and love.

The Holy Father has a profound understanding of the human person. That understanding seems to influence everything Pope Francis says. Cardinal Kaspar quotes the following from a speech Francis gave on November 30, 2014:

"Meeting each other, seeing each other face to face, exchanging the embrace of peace, and praying for each other, are all essential aspects of our journey toward the restoration of full communion. All of this precedes and always accompanies that other essential aspect of this journey, namely, theological dialogue. An authentic dialogue is, in every case,

---

[40] Ibid., p. 45.

an encounter between persons with a name, a face,
a past, and not merely a meeting of ideas." [41]

I think personalist philosophers such as Buber, Mounier, Marcel, and Clarke would applaud such a statement.

Francis' vision of the human person reveals the insightful humanism of the Holy Father. Often today, when people use the term humanism they mean secular or atheistic humanism. In fact, that is the way that I frequently use the term in the philosophy courses that I teach at St. John's University. Of course, that is not Pope Francis' humanism. Rather the Pope's vision of human nature is tied to belief in God and the mystery of human persons' relationship to God. There is no such reality as an unimportant person. It is obvious that Francis believes this deeply. There is no person who does not have a special gift to give. This is how God has created us. To be a human person is to be called to be a gift-giver. This is one of the most profound truths about a human person. When people meet one another in an atmosphere of mutual respect and openness to God's grace, amazing and marvelous things can happen.

I love Francis' reference to the uniqueness and history of each individual. A person's background and history can have an enormous influence on how the person thinks and judges. When people come together in a spirit of prayer, the Holy Spirit is present and what might initially seem impossible may become possible. The ecumenical movement is a wonderful example of how prayerful meetings can remove obstacles that may have seemed insurmountable. When I was a student in

---

[41] Ibid., p. 54.

the major seminary, a classmate arranged a meeting between some of our classmates and young men who were studying for ministry in other religious denominations. The meeting was wonderful. I had never previously had a discussion with people studying in other Christian denominations. I have taught at Princeton Theological Seminary, at Brooklyn College, Queens College, and at New York University. My experience of other professors and of students who did not share my faith was always an enlightening experience for me. I treasure those experiences.

Probably more than most priests in my more than fifty-six years as a priest, I have been involved with what seems like countless discussion groups. As a parish priest, I was involved with more than twenty groups. For the last thirty years I have met with a group of priests five or six times a year and with a group of lay people almost once a month. These meetings are one of the great blessings of my life. At each meeting, I discover again Francis' description of people —everyone has a name, a face, a past. Each is a gift-giver and I am the recipient of their gifts, of their insights, and their goodness.

Pope Francis seems to be in his own life what he is teaching all of us to be. He is calling us to be people deeply aware of God's love for us and for everyone. The way Francis meets others, and thinks of others and speaks about others seems to make him a channel of God's grace. He is a light in the world. A priest friend of mine told me how grateful he is to God that he has lived to experience Francis' pontificate. I feel the same gratitude.

Discussion Questions

1. Is it realistic to hope for a "revolution of love"?

2. What insights of Cardinal Kaspar into Pope Francis' thought do you find most interesting? Most challenging?

3. What does it mean to read "the signs of the times"?

4. What do you think Cardinal Kaspar is referring to when, in comparing Pope Francis' theological method and emphasis to those of Pope Benedict, he claims Francis' method and emphasis are more kerygmatic and less didactic?

5. Do you agree that there is a lack of joy in the contemporary world? Why or why not?

6. Kaspar says that by "Gospel," Pope Francis does not mean a written document. What does Kaspar think Francis means?

7. Why should the Church herself be evangelized?

8. What do you think Pope Francis means by "a mysticism of coexistence"?

Chapter Five

Consumerism: The Objectification of Persons

Pope Francis has made so many statements about the evil of consumerism that his remarks have led me back to a book that I read several years ago, a book that profoundly influenced my outlook on society. The book is by John F. Kavanaugh, S.J., *Following Christ in a Consumer Society: The Spirituality of Cultural Resistance*. [42] I doubt if there is anything in Father Kavanaugh's book with which Pope Francis would disagree. Before I read his book, I had heard John give a few lectures on consumerism. He was a brilliant speaker, both informative and inspiring. The times that I heard him speak, I was not the only person to be impressed with his presentation. The reactions to his lectures seemed to be unanimously positive. When his book appeared, I knew I had to read it. Commenting on the loss of interior life in our society and calling attention to the loss of our personhood, Kavanaugh writes:

"No matter where we turn — to ourselves, to others or to society at large — we find personal reality

---

[42] John F. Kavanaugh, S.J., *Following Christ in a Consumer Society: The Spirituality of Cultural Resistance*, (New York, Maryknoll: Orbis, 1991), p. 194.

overshadowed by the omnipresent immensity of objects, whether it is in producing them, buying them, amassing them, or relating to them.

"The Consumer Society is a formation system; it forms us and our behavior. It is also an information system: it informs us as to our identity and as to the status of our world. Its influence is felt in every dimension of our lives and each dimension echoes and mirrors the others. The individual's 'lost self' is paralleled in the dissolution of mutuality and relationship. The personal and interpersonal breakdown is reflected in the social economic worlds through a general socialized degradation of persons, through flight from human vulnerability, especially found in marginal people, and through a channeling of human desire into the amassing of possessions." [43]

What makes John's insights seem to me even more relevant today than when he wrote them is my observation of people using cell phones and other relatively new gadgets to "communicate" with other persons. I put the word communicate in quotation marks because I fear that all these new gadgets are not really fostering communication. When I walk from my office in the building at St. John's University that houses the philosophy department to my classes in another building, I probably pass about thirty to forty students. No student makes eye contact. Everyone, and I mean everyone, is on some kind of gadget. Even more amazing to me is the presence of cell phones in other social situations. One of the most discouraging scenes I have seen

---

[43] Ibid., p. 4.

more than once is two people sitting at the same table in a restaurant and each is on a cell phone. I have a vivid memory of driving in a car with a man who called his wife about fifteen times in less than an hour. Many of my friends seem to keep in contact through phones most of the day. If they are not on their phones speaking with or texting someone, they are checking their messages. Why must there be what seems like constant contact? What does this kind of pressure to be in touch with others do to us? Is our ability to relate to other persons improving because of contemporary technology or is the opposite happening? Are these tools of communication helping us to relate interpersonally with one another or are they merely fostering shallow communication? What Father Kavanaugh stresses in his book is the danger that objects are becoming more important than persons. There is a great danger that people are judged in terms of the things they own. Pope Francis is calling us to reflect profoundly and prayerfully on what we value most in our lives and in our societies.

Recently, I reread some of the pages near the beginning of Father John Kavanaugh's book. These pages are the beginning of his analysis of the problems with a consumer society, and what living in a consumer society can do to us. The Jesuit priest's insights at first upset me and then challenged me. Father Kavanaugh suggests that there is a hole in the center of what he calls "the consuming self." We are in danger of losing our interior life. We can be seduced into living only for appearances. Father Kavanaugh writes the following description of the "consuming self":

"There is no substance to our being, nothing there but the appearances, the 'outside,' the 'looking good'. . . . There is a hole underneath it all. It is a discovery frighteningly made in those moments of true solitude when we are no longer producing, consuming, marketing, or buying . . .

'The flight from the solitary personal self, haunts our compulsion to work, our urgency to produce. We often seem incapable of living in the present moment while paradoxically we feel robbed of time." [44]

What really speaks to me is Father Kavanaugh's remark about the need to live in the present moment. One interest that many psychologists and psychiatrists have when they interview people is to see if the person can live in the present. If the person is depressed this could be a sign of living in the past; if the person is anxious, it could be a sign that the person is living in the future. To be able to live in the present moment is a sign of mental and emotional health. Not only is living in the present moment a sign of emotional health, but it is also related to an important truth in ascetical theology. Theologians talk about the grace of the present moment. God is always present to us. We may forget about God, but God never forgets about us. God's presence keeps us in existence and God's presence can enable us to grow into a deeper relationship with God.

I am a person who tends to be anxious. This goes back at least to my high school days. Back then, it took the form of extreme scrupulosity. I had an erroneous

---

[44] Ibid., p. 6.

notion of what was and was not sinful and that was accompanied by an image of a frightening God. I can recall how difficult receiving the sacrament of reconciliation was for me during high school. Today my anxiety focuses occasionally on church projects in which I am involved, essays I have to write or talks I have to give. None of these frightens me, but they can preoccupy me so that I am living more in the future than in the present moment even though everything I believe about God tells me that all these projects are more God's projects than mine.

I should trust more in God's presence and this could help me to have a more balanced outlook on any priestly work I try to do. Living in the present moment, resting, relaxing, and enjoying God's loving presence, may be the best antidote to the temptations of consumerism. Believing and trusting in God's loving presence would seem to be the exact opposite of trusting in things or appearances. If we are unconditionally loved by God, and we are, then why should we worry about how people judge us and evaluate us? We have been shown our value, dignity, and importance through the life, teaching, death and resurrection of God's Son.

Father Kavanaugh quotes a statement by Lee Atwater, a political and cultural strategist, after he discovered he had terminal brain cancer. The following is Atwater's statement:

> *"The '80s were about acquiring—acquiring wealth, power, prestige. I know. I acquired more wealth, power and prestige than most. But you can acquire all you want and still feel empty. What power wouldn't I pay for a little more time with my*

family! What price wouldn't I pay for an evening with friends! It took a deadly illness to put me eye to eye with that truth, but it is a truth that the country, caught up in its ruthless ambitions and moral decay, can learn on my dime. I don't know who will lead us through the 90s, but they must be made to speak to this spiritual vacuum at the heart of American society, this tumor of the soul." [45]

To the extent that I am in touch with the depth of my personhood, to that extent I can be open, honest, and real to another. And it is also true that to the extent that I am open and real in relation to another, to the extent that I present the real me and not just some facade that conceals my real identity, to that extent I am helped to be in touch with the depth of myself as a person. This amazes me. An intimate love relationship has enormous power to help persons grow as persons. Such a relationship can help us to *be* and not merely *seem*.

On every level of being human, we depend on one another. From food to clothing, from air travel to highways, and from medical treatment to entertainment, we are tied together. Philosophers use the word "co-exist" to indicate how we are related to one another. Of course, receiving food, clothing, and all the other ways that we depend on one another are important but I think that the most important way that we co-exist is implicit in the quotation from Kavanaugh about our interior lives.

I think that this vision of personal existence has important implications for how we relate to God. The

---

[45] Ibid., p. 7.

commandment to love one another is not an arbitrary commandment. Rather it is related to our deepest needs. It reveals to us what can help us grow as persons. We grow not only by being loved but also by loving.

Some of the most brilliant and insightful theologians whom I have read in the last five or ten years are convinced that in order to help people better understand Christian beliefs people have to be helped to ask important questions and to see how the answers to those questions should direct their lives. Reflection on what is important is not encouraged in our society. In fact, it may even be discouraged. At times contemporary society seems to be militantly opposed to any serious reflection.

About forty years ago, my confessor encouraged me to do centering prayer. I wonder if I have ever received more important advice. Spending fifteen or twenty minutes each day quietly thinking about God's presence within me seems to have helped me enormously. Though I still find it difficult to be still, certainly the time doing daily centering prayer has helped me to be a little less hyper. We have to battle the temptation to avoid thinking about what is most important and settling for the superficial and ephemeral. The scriptural injunction "Be still and know that I am God," could be used to build an entire spirituality, influencing our relationship with ourselves, with others, and especially with God. Being still could help us to know ourselves better and help us to grow in faith, hope, and love.

Put simply, I would say that a gospel tells us our identity, the identity of other persons and the identity of God. The gospel of consumerism tells us that we are consumers and that our value is in what we possess. It tells us that other persons are consumers and that we should want to have more than they do. It encourages us to not only "keep up with the Joneses" but to have more than the Joneses. It tells us that the "god" we should worship and serve is money, power, or possessions. Whichever gospel we follow will influence how we perceive everything and will greatly influence us in our choice of vocation. In fact, it will greatly influence much of our conduct.

The Christian gospel tells us that we exist because of God's free loving act of creating us. It tells us that we are unconditionally and unreservedly loved by God. We do not have to win this love, earn this love or merit this love. It is a gift. The Christian Gospel tells us that all persons are our brothers and sisters, also unconditionally loved by God. Because of their dignity, we should love them. Not only should we not do evil to them, but also when we can, we should be good to them. In Pope Francis' magnificent encyclical, *Laudato Si*, the Pope points out that all of us are related. The Christian gospel tells us that God's love for us is so great that we have been created for eternity, that God's love has conquered death.

The two gospels are so different that it is difficult to compare them. It is much easier to contrast them. The gospel of consumerism, if embraced and lived, will lead not to personal growth but more likely to selfishness and self-centeredness. It can even nourish narcissism. It can seduce us into looking for fulfillment and salvation where they cannot be found. No thing or set of things will ever fulfill us. We are created for love relationships. The Christian gospel, if embraced and lived, can change our view on everything. Romano Guardini expressed a profound truth when he said that a Christian climbs a tree differently. The Christian gospel sheds new light on all of reality.

Depth and the Human Person

When I first started teaching philosophy at St. John's University more than thirty years ago, I believed strongly in the benefits that a contemporary student might derive from studying philosophy. My own study of philosophy had convinced me that I knew some important truths, and I wanted to communicate those truths to others. I have never accepted the caricature of philosophy as an ethereal, excessively speculative and abstract study that has little if any importance in a person's life. That is certainly not a description of the philosophy of personalism. The study of philosophy, I believe, should be a life-changer. My own study of philosophy, both as an undergraduate and as a graduate student, enriched my life immeasurably. The many years that I have been teaching the philosophy of personalism have led to new insights into myself, into freedom, truth and love, and into the mystery of God.

Rereading Pope Francis has strengthened my commitment to challenge students in philosophy classes at St. John's. Studying philosophy is one way that we can enter more deeply into the interior depths of who we are. Much in our consumer society almost seems militant in discouraging deep reflection on what is most important in life. When we become aware of that, we should do what we can to avoid being seduced. Socrates was correct when he pointed out more than two thousand years ago that the unexamined life is not worth living.

If Pope Francis' analysis of contemporary society is correct, and I think it is, then we should take every opportunity to nourish our interior lives, either through religious practices such as prayer or through educational opportunities such as reading great literature or experiencing great art on the stage or screen or listening to great music. Any experience of depth should be welcomed. We may be hesitant to be in touch with the depth of ourselves, perhaps even a little frightened. Much in our consumer culture can distract us from reflecting on what is most important in our lives. When we do, seriously reflect on our existence, we may become aware of how finite and fragile we are. Such awareness can scare us. However, if we include in our reflection on ourselves awareness of the loving God Who keeps us in existence, Who died for us, Who lives within us, and Who constantly surrounds us with love, then what was initially frightening may appear absolutely marvelous and beautiful.

Pope Francis is calling us to what Father Kavanaugh calls a covenantal relationship. In Father Kavanaugh's words:

> "A covenantal relationship is a mutual commitment of self-donation between free beings capable of self-conscious reflection and self-possession. Covenant as the free gift of self, the promising of oneself, is a characteristic unique to such free beings." [46]

---

[46] Ibid., p. 65.

I have come to believe that a covenantal relationship is the way to have a fulfilling human life. We have been created in order to have covenantal relationships. Though it said this in different words, this is what the penny catechism taught. Every person is meant by his or her very nature to be a gift-giver. This is how we have been made by God. To give oneself to another or others in a covenantal relationship is the way to personal fulfillment. A consumer culture tells us almost the complete opposite of this profound truth about ourselves. It tells us that fulfillment and happiness lie in possessing more and more things. This is not true. No thing or set of things will ever fulfill us. We are created for interpersonal relationships and a covenantal relationship is the highest type of personal relationship.

Father Kavanaugh sketches a philosophy of person that he thinks applies to all persons. In reading his insights, I was delighted to rediscover what I had read in his book many years ago: Father Kavanaugh's philosophy of person is basically the same as the philosophy of person that I teach to students at St. John's University. Father Kavanaugh points to the universal experience of human beings that they are unfinished, incomplete. He writes the following:

"This incompleteness is expressed in a striving for, a being driven to, the realization of our potentialities in a mutuality of knowing and loving. Conditioned and limited goals or goods serve not as final satisfactions for our striving so much as they constitute continual reminders of its apparent insatiability and inexhaustibility. The dynamics and structure of consciousness indicate that our very

> *'being' is a calling out for fullness, a being-toward,'*
> *a grand historical longing, a stretching out beyond*
> *the mere givenness of our limits. What is, is surely*
> *often lovely, but never enough. Thus, men and*
> *women question. And in doing so, they posit the*
> *quandary that is one with their identity as persons:*
> *Why are they not sufficient to themselves?"* [47]

I agree completely with Father Kavanaugh's analysis of the human person's striving for fulfillment. To make his description real for ourselves all we need do is look at our experience. For example, I am told about some new, great movie. I see it and even agree that it is great, but it does not fulfill me completely. I am told about a new book, which some critics describe as a masterpiece. I read the book and agree that it is a masterpiece, but I am still not fulfilled. I eagerly look forward to some event that I think is going to be incredibly enjoyable. The event comes and it is enjoyable but it does not fulfill me completely. I immediately look toward the future for some new experience. Even experience of the presence of friends and loved ones, probably the best experience that anyone of us has, does not fulfill us completely.

What disturbs me a great deal is that large numbers of people who seem to have no religious faith do not ask questions about why there is a lack in their lives or what is the point and goal of human living. What is happening that somehow so many people no longer ask the big questions: Why am I here, what does my journey through life mean and does it have any significance? That they have no answer is sad, but even more

---

[47] Ibid., p. 67.

disturbing is their apparent lack of interest in the questions.

It is not easy to face our mortality, our finitude, and fragility. We want to forget about it and so we substitute other activity in place of serious reflection. Yet I have become convinced that if we are going to allow ourselves to be fulfilled and to experience the deepest joy of living, we have to deal intelligently and correctly with our mortality. Running away from it is neither correct nor intelligent. Ultimately, it is not even possible. I suggest that the most intelligent way of dealing with our mortality is through living out in our daily lives the mystery of love. The most profound way of living out in our daily lives the mystery of love, I believe, is through Christian faith and commitment.

I have come to see in a new way that our very weakness is our strength; our neediness is essential to our being who we are; our poverty is ultimately our wealth. The new way of viewing our fragility, finitude, and morality is partly due to my reading of Pope Francis. In trying to explain this, I have to appeal to two mysteries, perhaps the two most profound mysteries in our experience: the mysteries of our unfinishedness and the mystery of God's unlimited love of us.

God has creatively fashioned us so that our deepest selves long for God, are directed toward God, can only be fulfilled by a love relationship with God. This relationship will be completely fulfilled beyond the grave but here on earth a loving commitment to God is as close to heaven that we can come. That God has made us, so that only through a relationship with God can we be fulfilled, is not a selfish act by God. Rather it is a most unselfish act because God creates us this way for our benefit. I ask myself, why would God, the Infinite God, Who keeps the stars, planets, and millions of other creatures in existence, want a love relationship with Bob Lauder? The only answer I can give is that love is giving. When humans act unselfishly, they are imitating God. We do not have to deny or run away from our fragility and finitude. Rather serious reflection on how needy we are may help us to appreciate God's love more. Serious reflection on our fragility and finitude when linked to prayerful reflection on Jesus' death and resurrection may lead us to a deeper realization of just how important we are to God. Facing our poverty in being may help us to discern our richness as beloved by God. If we follow Pope Francis' plea that we face our poverty, we may discover our wealth as God's beloved.

Discussion Questions

1. What do you think "the gospel of consumerism" is?

2. Is our ability to communicate helped or hindered by contemporary technology?

3. What do you think of Father Kavanaugh's emphasis on the importance of living in the present moment?

4. Does Atwater's statement (p. 81) speak to you and your experience in the contemporary world?

5. Do you think contemporary society is opposed to serious reflection?

Chapter Six

A Most Important Encyclical

Pope Francis' encyclical, *Laudato Si*,[48] is so important that it deserves an entire book. Because of the letter's length, it took me several hours to read it. Having finished reading it, I wonder if there could ever be a better way of spending those hours. Though demanding, the encyclical is absolutely beautiful.

As enthusiastic as I am about the encyclical, I was slightly surprised when I recently heard an outstanding Catholic theologian comment, "I think this is the most important encyclical ever." I thought of some of the great social encyclicals from the past, and also on Pope Benedict's marvelous encyclical on love. When questioned about the comment, the theologian said, "Because it involves the lives of millions of people," meaning that millions will die if we do not take care of the environment.

Early in the encyclical, (paragraph five), Pope Francis writes:

> *"All authentic human development has a moral character. It presumes full respect for the human*

---

[48] Pope Francis, Apostolic Exhortation of the Holy Father, *Laudato Si: On Care for Our Common Home*, (Indiana: Our Sunday Visitor Publishing Division, 2015), p. 176.

person, but it must also be concerned for the world around us. . . . Accordingly, our human ability to transform reality must proceed in line with God's original gift of all that is." [49]

I was surprised by some of the comments from Catholics indicating that they could not see how morality extended to how we treat the environment. Such comments are discouraging because they reveal that much education about the role of the Church in the world still has to take place. The Pope's teaching in the encyclical and in other statements has given me a new and deeper understanding of what it means to say that to be a human person is to be relational, to be in dialogue with other, present to other, open to other. I have come to see through the Holy Father that not only how we relate to other persons is important, but that it is also important how we relate to all other creatures.

With this broadening of my understanding of how humans should be relating, my memory has gone back to my undergraduate education. Of course, memory can play tricks on us, but I do not think that in any of my undergraduate philosophy or theology courses there was a great emphasis on the meaning of person as relational. There also was a lack of emphasis on how we experience ourselves and others. I think the word *"experience"* during the four years that I studied undergraduate theology was used once in a theology class. I am not complaining or blaming anyone. Theology, like any other study engaged in by human beings, either improves and deepens or, unfortunately, perhaps

---

[49] Ibid., (par. 5), p. 9.

becomes shallow and narrow. I think that the words "*a human person's nature is to be relational*" sums up as well as any other expression the nature or essence of a human person. What the Holy Father has done for me and I hope for many, is to point out that how we relate to non-human realities, in other words to nature, is extremely important. Commenting on St. Francis of Assisi, Pope Francis writes the following:

> "*. . . Saint Francis is the exemplar par excellence of care for the vulnerable and of an integral ecology lived out joyfully and authentically. He is the patron saint of all who study and work in the area of ecology, and he is also much loved by non-Christians. He was particularly concerned for God's creation and for the poor and outcast. He loved, and was deeply loved for his joy, his generous self-giving, his openheartedness. He was a mystic and a pilgrim who lived in simplicity and in wonderful harmony with God, with others, with nature and with himself. He shows us just how inseparable the bond is between concern for nature, justice for the poor, commitment to society, and interior peace.*" [50]

One of the goals in my life, at least since my college years, has been to integrate all my experiences around my religious faith. When I was a college student, I met a Catholic who I thought had succeeded in doing that in his life. I was deeply impressed and wanted to imitate him, though I probably have failed more than I have succeeded. Pope Francis has now offered to me and to others a profound understanding of Catholic faith as an integral force in a person's life. I believe that the Holy

---

[50] Ibid., (par. 10), p. 12.

Father is correct in claiming that there is a bond between concern for nature, justice for the poor, commitment to society, and interior peace. His wonderful vision of reality inspires me and encourages me to continue to seek a profound integrity in my life with my Catholic faith as the central integrating force.

I find the Pope's writing both beautiful and inspiring. Early in the letter, Pope Francis reveals his appreciation of God's creation. The Holy Father writes the following:

> *"It is not enough, however, to think of different species merely as potential 'resources' to be exploited, while overlooking the fact that they have value in themselves. Each year sees the disappearance of thousands of plant and animal species which we will never know, which our children will never see, because they have been lost forever. The great majority become extinct for reasons related to human activity. Because of us, thousands of species will no longer give glory to God by their very existence, nor convey their message to us. We have no such right."* [51]

Pope Francis' vision, and it is a magnificent vision, includes every creature brought into existence by God. It is as though God is sending us a word or a message through the beings that God creates. Everything that God creates resembles God in some way. Each being is one, true, good, and beautiful. Philosophers call these the transcendentals. They characterize every being from cockroaches to angels. God cannot create anything that does not in some way resemble God. Pope Francis sees the beauty of God's creation. He sees deeply into

---

[51] Ibid., (par. 33), p. 26.

the goodness of creation and is profoundly saddened by what we are doing to our planet. The words of poet Gerard Manley Hopkins, S.J. come to mind: *"The world is charged with the grandeur of God."* [52]

A Universal Communion

One of the great insights of contemporary thought is that to be a person is to be relational. We can decide *how* we will relate, but we cannot decide *whether* we will relate. God has made us relational beings. Pope Francis is trying to expand our vision and deepen our sense that we are called to relate not only to other human persons and to God but also to all beings on our planet. In trying to expand our vision, the Pope is trying to expand and deepen our conscience. The definition of conscience that I use in philosophy courses at St. John's University is the following: A conscience is the habitual way that a human consciousness judges in moral matters. A very important word in that definition is "habitual." A conscience is a habit. It is not easy to change a conscience. We tend to make the same moral judgments for many years. Though a conscience should be deepening and broadening, it can become set, settled and even static. The Holy Father is trying to give us a truly global conscience, a conscience that sees that we are responsible not just for ourselves and our neighbors, but also for the material universe.

Pope Francis points out that the Book of Genesis in symbolic and narrative language contains profound

---

[52] Gerard Manley Hopkins, "God's Grandeur," in *The Poems of Gerard Manley Hopkins*, (Fourth Edition. Edited by W.H. Gardner and N.H. MacKenzie. New York: Oxford University Press, 1967), p. 66.

teachings about three fundamental relationships, namely, our relationship with God, our relationship with our neighbor, and our relationship with the earth. The Holy Father writes:

> *"Disregard for the duty to cultivate and maintain a proper relationship with my neighbor, for whose care and custody I am responsible, ruins my relationship with my own self, with others, with God and with the earth. When all those relationships are neglected, when justice no longer dwells in the land, the Bible tells us that life itself is endangered."* [53]

Pope Francis points out that there is

> *" . . . a conviction which we today share, that everything is interconnected, and that genuine care for our own lives and our relationships with nature is inseparable from fraternity, justice and faithfulness to others."* [54]

There are so many wonderful insights in the Pope's letter that, as I re-read it, I have the feeling that I can delve deeper and deeper into all the truths that the Holy Father is stressing. All creatures can speak to us of God, and how we relate to them can help us see not only more deeply into them, but also more deeply into ourselves. All creatures are so connected that how we relate to others, either causes us to grow or to decline.

God's creatures are precious gifts to us from God. The proper response to a gift is gratitude. We are called, not just to articulate the words "Thank You," but also to

---

[53] *Laudato Si*, op. cit., (par. 70), p. 51.
[54] Ibid.

live in such a way that our very life is a "Thank You."
To be able to live that way is another gift from God.

The Holy Father's vision is simultaneously challenging and inspiring, profound and yet accessible. My
experience in rereading Francis' letter has been encouraging, but also a little frightening. If the Pope's
thoughts on the environment are correct, and I think
they are, then action is necessary. There should be no
delay. God has made us responsible for the environment. Francis writes the following:

> *"In the Judeo-Christian tradition, the word 'cre-
> ation' has a broader meaning than 'nature,' for it
> has to do with God's loving plan in which every
> creature has its own value and significance. Nature
> is usually seen as a system which can be studied,
> understood and controlled, whereas creation can
> only be understood as a gift from the outstretched
> hand of the Father of all, and as reality illuminat-
> ed by the love which calls us together into universal
> communion."* [55]

Francis stresses that creation is a free choice, that it
does not come about in order to show force or as a need
or desire for self-assertion. Rather creation is due to
God's love, which is the basic moving force in all created things. When we ask why God creates, the only
answer we can come up with is that love shares. Nature
is not divine, but nevertheless, we should see that we
are responsible to treat nature properly. Francis sees
excitement and drama in human history precisely
because we can either use our freedom to nurture
nature or to cause setbacks. God's gift of freedom can be

[55] Ibid., (par. 76), p. 54.

used properly or improperly. The personalism of Pope Francis shines through his document. Pointing out that through creation there is a call from a "thou" to another "thou," Francis insists that we should see each human person as a subject who cannot ever be reduced to an object, but he also insists that other living beings should not be looked upon as mere objects, which we can arbitrarily dominate. Warning against any tyrannical domination by humans over other creatures, Francis writes the following:

> *"The ultimate purpose of other creatures is not to be found in us. Rather, all creatures are moving forward with us towards a common point of arrival, which is God, in that transcendent fullness where the risen Christ embraces and illumines all things. Human beings, endowed with intelligence and love, and drawn by the fullness of Christ, are called to lead all creatures back to their Creator."* [56]

The encyclical in a very profound way calls us to be Christocentric, to form our conscience by imitating Christ's love. Christ embraces all of creation and offers it back to his Father. Francis is calling us to imitate that embrace and to join in Christ's offering. This is what we do in every celebration of the Eucharist. We are called to treat non-human creatures with love and gratitude because they are precious gifts from God. What we do at a Eucharist should influence the way we live. It takes a long time to shape and form a conscience. Actually, it takes a lifetime and many realities to affect a conscience: from family to schools attended, from books read to films viewed, from the media to the

---

[56] Ibid., (par. 83), p. 58

Sunday homily. Francis' challenge to our consciences is marvelous. Today, Catholics are blessed to have a leader whose vision of the world is magnificent. Catholics should welcome Francis' leadership and allow his vision to deeply influence their consciences. It seems as though Francis' influence is not limited to Catholics, but is both challenging and encouraging to many who are not Catholic.

What I find most challenging but also exceptionally beautiful is the notion of "universal communion." There is no such reality as an unimportant person. Francis' personalistic view of creation suggests that a human person has the capacity to relate to all of reality. We are the guardians of creation. How we relate to other creatures will either lead to a beautiful future or contribute significantly to a destructive future. The future is not something that merely happens to us but rather something that we, to some extent, create by our free choices. Universal communion provides an image of the human person motivated by love and gratitude for God's gift of creation, treating all beings with respect. All of creation is a message of love from God. To disregard that message, to deliberately misuse God's gifts is sinful. I think of St. Thérèse's statement: *"all is grace."* [57] That, I think, is part of Francis' message in *Laudato Si,* The more we love and respect God's creations, the more deeply we will see into them and see God's presence in them. In the encyclical, Pope Francis claims that humanity has dealt with technology and its development according to a one-dimensional model. According

[57] St. Thérèse of Lisieux. *Her Last Conversations*. Translated from the original manuscripts by John Clarke, O.C.D., Institute for Carmelite Studies: Washington, DC, 1977, p. 57.

to this model, a person is exalted who uses logical and rational procedures to exercise control over the object while neglecting the possibilities inherent in the thing itself. If this is the way we approach nature and deal with nature, we are misusing one of God's great gifts to us. The way we deal with nature tells us something about how we view God as well as how we view nature and ourselves. Francis writes the following:

> *"Neglecting to monitor the harm done to nature and the environmental impact of our decisions is only the most striking sign of a disregard for the message contained in the structures of nature itself. When we fail to acknowledge as part of reality the worth of a poor person, a human embryo, a person with disabilities — to offer just a few examples— it becomes difficult to hear the cry of nature itself, everything is connected."* [58]

If I had to sum up the Holy Father's encyclical in one sentence, the sentence would be "Everything is connected." That statement is the prism through which Francis views everything. The Paschal Event changes everything. It both challenges us and comforts us. It reveals that all persons are brothers and sisters, loved and redeemed by God. It calls our attention to the dignity and importance of every person. It reminds us of how much everyone is loved by God. Pope Francis writes:

> *"Our openness to others, each of whom is a 'thou' capable of knowing, loving and entering into dialogue, remains the source of our nobility, as humans. A correct relationship with the created world demands that we not weaken this social*

---

[58] *Laudato Si*, op. cit., (par. 117), p. 79.

dimension of openness to others, much less the transcendent dimension of our openness to the "Thou" of God. Our relationship with the environment can never be isolated from our relationship with others and with God. Otherwise, it would be nothing more than romantic individualism dressed up in ecological garb, locking us into stifling immanence." [59]

I love the way Pope Francis in his encyclical ties together our relationship with one another to our relationship with God, and our relationship with God and with one another to our relationship with all of creation. To look deeply into the mystery of the human person is to see the face of our neighbors and also the face of God, in whose image all of us have been created. The Holy Father stresses our social obligations toward our brothers and sisters and toward the rest of creation in the light of the common good, a very important social principle that, unfortunately, seems to have been forgotten by many.

"Human ecology is inseparable from the notion of the common good, a central and unifying principle of social ethics. The common good is 'the sum of those conditions of social life which allow social groups and their individual members relatively thorough and ready access to their own fulfillment . . . [60]

" . . . In the present condition of global society, where injustices abound and growing numbers of people are deprived of basic human rights and con-

---

[59] Ibid., (par. 119), p. 81.
[60] Ibid., (par. 156), p. 104.

> sidered expendable, the principle of the common good immediately becomes, logically and inevitably, a summons to solidarity and a preferential option for the poorest of our brothers and sisters. This option entails recognizing the implications of the universal destination of the world's goods . . . it demands before all else an appreciation of the immense dignity of the poor in the light of our deepest convictions as believers. We need only look around us to see that, today, this option is in fact an ethical imperative essential for effectively attaining the common good." [61]

The expression of Pope Francis "the immense dignity of the poor in the light of our deepest convictions as believers" really speaks to me. I think that our Christian faith ought to shed light on all of our experience. In our society, we, through various media, receive many different images of the poor. Pope Francis reminds us that as believers we should be very aware of the immense dignity of the poor. The poor have immense dignity because they are persons and they have immense dignity because of Jesus dying for them. Whatever other images we might have of the poor, what Francis tells us is the bottom line.

The best essay that I have read about the encyclical was written by Rowan Williams, an Anglican prelate, theologian and poet, who was archbishop of Canterbury from 2002 to 2012. The essay, entitled "Embracing Our Limits: The Lessons of *Laudato Si*," appeared in the Oct. 9, 2015 issue of *Commonweal*. [62] In the early days

---

[61] Ibid., (par. 158), p. 105.
[62] Rowan Williams, "Embracing Our Limits: The Lessons of *Laudato Si*," *Commonweal*, Oct. 9, 2015, pp. 13-15.

of his pontificate, Francis seemed to be very different from his papal predecessors. Of course, like everyone else, Francis is a unique personality and to some extent he reveals a little of that personality in everything he says and does. But in terms of his teaching, I do not think he has ever said anything that contradicts any doctrine that any other Pope has taught. What may seem different in teaching I believe is a question of emphasis. At the beginning of his essay, Rowan Williams writes the following:

> *"Perhaps the first thing that needs to be said about Pope Francis' encyclical on the environment is that it is an entirely natural development not only of the theology of* Evangelii Gaudium, *but also—as the extensive citations show—of the theology of Pope Benedict, especially as found in* Caritas in Veritate. *Both the pope's critics and his supporters have often missed the point: Benedict's Christian humanism, his consistent theology of the dignity of the human person, his concern for a culture in which there is no longer a viable understanding of any given order independent of human will—all this is reiterated with force and clarity by Pope Francis."* [63]

Williams goes on to say that we live in a culture that seems to be deaf to any sense of natural law and that some seem to think that mere personal desire is the only "given" in the universe. They think that the only source of morality is what we desire so that nothing else informs us or binds us. I agree with Francis' and Rowan's indictment of a culture that has lost any sense

---

[63] Ibid., p. 13.

that ethical meanings can be found by reflecting on human nature. Williams is both strong and clear in his indictment of the view that we are the total source of meaning that the universe is subject to our wishes and whims. He writes the following:

> *"The material world tells us that to be human is to be in dialogue with what is other: what is physically other, what is humanly other in the solid three-dimensionality of other persons, ultimately what is divinely other. And in a world created by the God Christians believe in, this otherness is always communicating: meaning arises in this encounter, it is not devised by our ingenuity. Hence the pope's significant and powerful appeal to be aware of the incalculable impact of the loss of biodiversity; it is not only a loss of resource but a diminution of meaning."* [64]

Williams' insistence that Francis' teaching is a development of Benedict's teaching is important. Catholic teaching always involves mystery and so we can always go more deeply into Christian truth. The deeper we go, the more marvelous the truth about God and the truth about us seems. Everything we believe about God ultimately tells us something about the mystery of love.

One of the nicest bonuses for me in studying the encyclical *Laudato Si* has been to discover that the philosophy of person that underlies Francis' vision is basically the same as the philosophy I teach students at St. John's University. It is nice to discover that in the philosophy of person that we embrace, the Holy Father and I seem to be on the same page.

---

[64] Ibid.

In his excellent essay, Rowan Williams states succinctly a vision of what it means to be a human in the world. Williams writes the following:

> "*The argument of these opening sections of* Laudato Si *repeatedly points us back to a fundamental lesson: We as human beings are not the source of meaning or value; if we believe we are, we exchange the real world for a virtual one, a world in which—to echo Lewis Carroll's Humpty Dumpty— the only question is who is to be master. A culture in which managing limits is an embarrassing and unwelcome imperative is a culture that has lost touch with the very idea of a world, let alone a created world (i.e. one in which a creative intelligence communicates with us and leads us into meanings and visions we could not have generated ourselves).*" [65]

Williams stresses that one of the encyclical's underlying issues is the loss of meaning. A culture that believes that the human person is the total source of meaning can justify just about anything that seems convenient to a person.

I was delighted to read the praise that Williams bestows on the thinker whom, apart from previous Popes, Francis most often quotes in the encyclical. Apparently, the great German theologian, Romano Guardini, has been a strong influence on Francis' thinking. As I have mentioned previously, when I was in the major seminary as a student in the 50s, one of the spiritual authors who was very popular among seminarians was Guardini. I do not know who is reading him

---

[65] Ibid.

today but my guess is that as his influence on Pope Francis' thinking becomes better known, we will see a revival of interest in this truly great theologian. As I write this, I am thinking of how much I profited from Guardini's insights, which seemed to leap off the page at me. Williams suggests that Guardini represents the ecclesially and liturgically informed theology, which came to fruition just before Vatican II. He thinks that Guardini's theology *"presents a coherent, imaginatively vivid, socially and politically critical worldview profoundly rooted in a highly traditional dogmatics, looking back to those patristic and monastic sources in which ethics, liturgy, spirituality, and doctrine were not separated."* [66]

Emphasizing that Pope Francis' thought is a development of Pope Benedict's, Williams notes that Guardini was also admired by Benedict. What I recall vividly from my reading of Guardini many years ago is both the depth and clarity of his writing. That Rowan Williams, the distinguished Anglican former archbishop of Canterbury, is enthusiastic about Francis' encyclical, I find encouraging for several reasons. One is that Williams is an excellent theologian. Another is that his enthusiasm bodes well for the ecumenical movement. This is how Williams ends his essay:

> *"The Pope's Cultural Revolution is about restored relationship with the creation we belong with and the creator who made us to share his bliss in communion; it is about the unbreakable links between contemplation, Eucharist, justice, and social transformation. It constitutes a major contribution to the*

---

[66] Ibid., p. 15.

ongoing unfolding of a body of coherent social teaching, and a worthy expansion and application of the deeply impressive doctrinal syntheses of Pope Benedict's major encyclicals." [67]

I think Williams makes an especially important point in describing the links between contemplation, Eucharist, justice and social transformation as "unbreakable." There should be a profound relation between contemplation and Eucharist, each nourishing the other. Both should lead to justice and social transformation. Williams is correct to state that the Holy Father is working toward a cultural revolution. The Pope's vision is appealing because it is so beautiful. It speaks to the deepest needs and desires of people.

---

[67] Ibid.

Discussion Questions

1. Is Pope Francis' encyclical *Laudato Si* a political statement? Why or why not?

2. How can we integrate our faith with all our knowledge? Do you have a favorite Catholic magazine?

3. Do you find your conscience changing often? If it does change, what causes it to change?

4. What do you think of Pope Francis' idea that "everything is connected"?

5. What do you think of the Pope's insistence that our treatment of the environment is connected to our relationship to God?

Chapter Seven

Mercy

Commenting on the parable of the steward who after being forgiven by his master refuses to forgive a subordinate, Sebastian Moore writes:

> *"The truth this parable is getting at in its deceptively simple fairy-story way is the existential truth that lies at the heart of the human condition: that my hardness of heart in respect of my* brother disguises from me *the fact that I am enormously in God's debt. Instead of saying* 'although I have been let off a huge debt, I won't even let someone else off a small one', *I should say* 'because I see no reason to remit my brother's debt, the forgiveness of God has no serious meaning for me.'*

> *"This turns the whole thing upside down. Far from refusal to remit being manifestly outrageous to me in the light of God's forgiveness of me, it is my refusal that is preventing the light from getting through...*

> *"We have to think of God's forgiveness as a transformation of consciousness."* [68]

---

[68] Moore, op cit, p. 82.

Moore's insight seems to me to be important. How we relate to other people influences how we relate to God. In the parable, the refusal to forgive blinds the person to the great gift of God's forgiveness. I have often observed how a person who holds a grudge is being hurt more than the person who needs forgiveness. In some cases, perhaps in all, the person who refuses to forgive is more needy and wounded than the person who needs forgiveness. In God's plan we really are tied together, our relationships with one another greatly influence our relationship with God. Examining my conscience, I have become aware of how long I nurture hurt feelings. I do not think, except in my fantasies, that I try to get even, that I try to pay back for the hurt I have experienced, but even that I might fantasize about "getting even" indicates that I have not really forgiven, that I have not put the experience of being hurt behind me. As long as I do not let go of my hurt feelings, to that extent I do not allow God to heal me.

Though I find Moore's book difficult reading, I also find it very provocative. Moore writes the following about forgiveness:

> "It touches not the self-important sinner but the sin of self-importance.
>
> "In touching this sin, the divine forgiveness is not acting out of character with its infinite and beyond-me root. On the contrary, self-importance is properly dissolved by that infinite and luminous centre that is its ultimate corrective. What is meant by the divine forgiveness of sin is that God begins to be God in the small, mean life of the sinner." [69]

---

[69] Ibid., p. 86.

I love the expression "God begins to be God in the small mean life of the sinner." We allow God to enter in and to heal us, or to paraphrase Moore, we allow God to be God in our lives. God always deals with us as free persons. Our free acceptance of God's love is crucial. Our "yes" allows God to change us. If I ever meet Pope Francis, I am going to ask him if he has read Moore's book. That I read it and re-read it prior to reading Francis' *The Name of God is Mercy* [70] may have been providential. While Moore's book can be difficult, Pope Francis' can seem deceptively simple. The insights and depth of Moore's thinking is at least matched by the Holy Father. I knew as I was reading *The Name of God is Mercy*, that a second and perhaps a third reading would be wise.

St. Patrick's Cathedral in New York City recently underwent a thorough renovation, both inside and out, which took about two years. The job was well done. The Cathedral is now more beautiful than ever. The day I visited, the Cathedral was mobbed. My guess is that a few thousand people were visiting that same day. Some were lighting candles, others were pausing and perhaps praying at some of the side altars; some were visiting the chapel at which the Blessed Sacrament is kept. I have no idea how many of the people were believers and how many were merely curious to see how the renovation went. Of course, there is no way that I can know, but my suspicion is that most were believers. Many comported themselves as though a

---

[70] Pope Francis, *The Name of God Is Mercy: A Conversation with Andrea Tornielli*, (Translated from the Italian by Oonagh Stransky. New York: Random House, 2016), p. 151.

visit to the Cathedral was a religious act. When I knelt before the Blessed Sacrament next to a close friend, who just days before had asked me to pray for someone experiencing a terrible temptation, without speaking to one another, I knew we were praying for the same person. The atmosphere in the Cathedral and the proximity of my friend seemed to make the prayer special to me. Though it was an easy prayer to say, I was very aware of its importance.

Viewing the candles, the many crucifixes, the altars, each honoring a different saint and the crowds of people, I thought of a scene from an Ernest Hemingway novel. The novel was *The Sun Also Rises*. My recollection of the scene is that the main character, Jake Barnes, who I do not think was a Catholic, visits a church in Spain and is impressed by all the religious symbols and signs of people's faith, and he thinks to himself: "What a great religion!" That was how I felt at the Cathedral. Everything in the Cathedral that I observed that day, including the people who were visiting St. Pat's, spoke to me of faith. I said to my companions, "This experience should make us feel glad that we are Catholics." I experienced the joy that Francis encourages us to have as believers; a joy that he thinks will attract others.

There is a passage in Moore's book that has made me think about the profound mystery that each of us is. We can always go deeper and see more clearly as we reflect on our lives. My experience when I reflect on mystery is often as I become aware of something new, I simultaneously become aware of how little I understand completely. It is an experience that I would describe as a chiaroscuro, a mixture of light and darkness. A friend of mine, a psychotherapist, was in therapy for twenty years. One reason he stayed in therapy for so many years was that he found that it helped him to help others. I said to him, "After twenty years, what do you have left to talk about?" He responded, "There's always something."

The following passage in Moore's book set me thinking about the deep mystery that each one of us is:

> "Man has a secret operative in all he desires, wills, and creates. It is, that, finally, he does not believe in himself. Balancing all his achievements, there is the death-wish. The latter reaches, in times of crisis and decay . . . a dangerous degree of overtness. But even in the time of flowering it was there. Not only does man know that he will die. He lets this fact speak to him of the vanity of all that he strives for. . . .
>
> "But this will-not-to-be is no mere weakness. It resists *the power which calls man into being and which, in his consciousness, calls him to being, to identity, to personhood, to himself.* The will-not-to-be desires to undo the order of being that represents this power, to make it not the case that man is called to an ever-greater intensity of selfhood." [71]

Of course, to resist the "*power which calls him*" is to resist God. This, I suspect, is what all of us do. St. Paul wrote that the good he wanted to do, he did not do and the evil he did not want to do, he did. The quote from Moore can remind us that there are no unimportant

---

[71] Moore, op. cit., p. 13.

persons. There is no one who is not being called by God to full personhood. There is no one who is not involved in an ongoing dialogue with God, a dialogue that either leads to a deeper relationship or, unfortunately, to a distancing, a weakening of relationship. God is all for us, inviting us to a deeper level of living and loving. Pope Francis has told us this in almost everything he says or writes.

Though our culture does not encourage deep reflection about ourselves, or our lives, there are many ways that we can be counter-cultural and enter into deep reflection. I think education can help us do this. I suspect that listening to beautiful music can help us to be more reflective. Reading good magazines can help us to be more reflective about how we are directing our lives. The film festivals that I conduct are attempts to encourage people to see films that are great art and can lead to deep reflection. This is also the reason that I have been involved for thirty years in an adult education program centered on Catholic novels. Reading a great novel can broaden our horizons and set us thinking about what is most important in our lives. Submitting to spiritual direction with an intelligent spiritual director can help us. So can psychotherapy. I have come to believe that prayer can lead us into the depth of both God and ourselves. Perhaps this is the most important and effective way to grow as persons. What I think is that an honest, open presence to God is the most effective way to enter into the depth of our personhood.

Moore's insights expressed in the passage, remind us that God is not only not against us, but is trying to lead us to the fullness of personhood. This is the one truth about God that we try to express when we say that God is love. Listening to and reading Pope Francis' words can help us to be counter-cultural. Pope Francis has challenged the consciences not only of Catholics, but of just about everyone.

Mercy: God's Yes

I have the feeling that everything I have written about Pope Francis has been summed up in his book: *The Name of God Is Mercy: A Conversation With Andrea Tornielli*. In his introduction, entitled "To the Reader: Francis's Vision," [72] Tornielli summarizes Francis' view of mercy. He points out that for Pope Francis mercy is the Lord's strongest message, which is what Francis said in a homily about a week after his election. Certainly, his pontificate seems to be centered on the concept of mercy as shown by Jesus' teaching and healing and especially by his death and resurrection. The image of God that Francis presents again and again is that God is so in love with us that God cannot say "No" to us.

Tornielli comments on the difference between forgiveness and mercy in Francis' teaching. With forgiveness, our sins are removed. Mercy is more than just forgiveness. It represents the infinite love of God for us. It summarizes God's entire presence in our lives. Tornielli sees it as central to Francis' first few years as the leader of the Catholic Church. In reflecting on the Holy Father's message, Tornielli makes an important point about responsibilities. A special fault of our time seems to be the readiness to blame others, instead of ourselves.

---

[72] Pope Francis-Tornielli, op. cit., pp. ix-xx.

I found especially interesting Tornielli's report of a change that Francis wanted in the first draft of the text. In discussing ourselves as sinners, Tornielli reported Francis as saying "The medicine is there, the healing is there — if only we take a small step toward God." Francis called him and asked him to add "or even just the desire to take that step." I think that suggests Francis' idea that mercy is more than forgiveness. God's mercy meets us more than halfway. God's mercy is represented in the father's running to meet the prodigal son even before the son expresses that he has sinned against his father.

In trying to convey how mercy is a sign of God's infinite love of us, Francis refers to a novel by Bruce Marshall, *To Every Man a Penny*. [73] In the novel, a young priest has to hear the confession of a German soldier who is to be executed. The soldier confesses many sins against chastity and because he received great pleasure from those actions, he confesses that he cannot repent, and cannot say that he is sorry. The priest asks him if he can at least be sorry that he cannot repent. When the German soldier says that he is sorry that he cannot be sorry for his sins, the young priest absolves him. I have just put this novel on my list of books to read.

When I was a newly ordained priest, many years ago, in the parish in which I served, I heard confessions every week for about four-and-a-half hours. I loved the experience and had a very strong feeling that in the confessional I was being a priest in a special way. I never found hearing confessions a discouraging experi-

---

[73] Ibid., p. 7.

ence and I do not think I ever became angry with a penitent. Rather I found hearing confessions inspiring and encouraging. So many people trying to live morally and to grow closer to Christ! Recalling those years and the many hours in the confessional, I think the courses I took in moral theology as a student in the seminary helped me a great deal. Still I wish that in my education I had received the emphasis on mercy that Francis has frequently proclaimed. I believe that Francis' view of God's mercy comes out of the Holy Father's profound personalism, which springs from his deep awareness of God's personal loving presence in the life of everyone and the dignity and importance of every human being.

Several qualities make Francis attractive to both Catholics and others. His compassion is as obvious as his humility. His sense of humor and joy seem to spring from a profound peace, which in turn comes from his awareness of God's love for him, even though he readily admits he is a sinner.

When I first read *The Name of God Is Mercy*, I felt as though some of the ideas were very familiar to me because of other writings of Francis that I had read and other writings about him that I had read. Yet when I finished the book, I knew that I had to return to it. Almost instinctively, I sensed that I had missed some of Francis' most profound thoughts. My gut feeling was right. The book presents a very deep vision of God that, if embraced, could color one's whole relationship with God.

A theme that Pope Francis seems to return to frequently is that God is faithful. We can rely on God's love and commitment. God will never abandon us or forget us. We can rely on God's fidelity and love.

I think one of the most dramatic acts in any person's life, indeed perhaps the most dramatic act, is making a vow. Most Catholics have their baptismal vows made by godparents but at some time in their lives, they should make those vows their own. Two people making marriage vows I find an awesome act. The unconditional nature of the vow is both frightening and marvelous. Vows can be a great sign of love. People making religious vows of poverty, chastity and obedience, committing themselves to keep those vows for their entire lives, is awesome. But as awesome as human commitments are, the commitment that God makes to us, is almost incredibly awesome. The God Who creates us at every second of our life, has made a commitment to us so that we can count on Divine Love surrounding and supporting us throughout our lives. The God Who holds the universe in existence has made promises to us. If that is not awesome, then nothing is awesome.

We are surrounded by God's love when everything in our lives seems to be going smoothly; we are surrounded by God's love when nothing in our lives seems to be going well. Human beings sometimes break life commitments. God's commitment to us will never be broken. Mentioning how previous Popes such as Saint John XXIII, Paul VI, Saint John Paul II stressed mercy, Francis quotes Pope Benedict on the central role that mercy has in Divine revelation:

> *"Mercy is in reality the core of the Gospel message: it is the name of God himself, the face with which he revealed himself in the Old Testament and fully in Jesus Christ, incarnation of Creative and Redemptive Love. This love of mercy also illu-*

*minates the face of the Church, and is manifested
through the Sacraments, in particular that of
Reconciliation, as well as in works of charity, both
of community and individuals. Everything that the
Church says and does shows that God has mercy
for man."* [74]

There is an anecdote that Francis tells that I found
especially touching. It reveals the simple but strong
faith of a Capuchin priest but also the humanism and
deep vision into the goodness of persons that charac-
terizes Francis' personalism. In Buenos Aires Francis
met a Capuchin priest who had a reputation as a great
confessor. The priest had come to Francis because he
was concerned that in the many confessions he heard
he was too lenient. He had doubts that he perhaps had
forgiven too much. Francis asked him what he did
when he had these doubts. The Capuchin said he went
into the chapel and stood before the tabernacle and
asked Jesus to forgive him if he had forgiven too much.
But then, the Capuchin said to Jesus that it was He
who set the bad example! I love that anecdote. It
reveals not only the goodness and faith of the Capuchin
but also the goodness and faith of the Holy Father.

Another anecdote that Francis tells I also found moving. Francis' niece was married to a man in a civil
union. They were planning to celebrate the sacrament
of marriage after the man received his annulment. The
man went to Mass every Sunday and went into the confessional. He told the priest that he knew that he could
not be absolved but that he would like the priest to give
him a blessing. In light of the man's practice of attend-

---
[74] Ibid., pp. 12-13.

ing Mass and explaining in the confessional his situation and then asking for a blessing, Francis believes that the man was a religiously mature person. I do too. I hope I have these two anecdotes on my mind the next time I hear confessions.

I can recall with some accuracy when Catholics began to stop celebrating the Sacrament of Reconciliation. When I went away to graduate school in 1964, there were still confession lines every Saturday afternoon in church. When I returned in 1967, many of my friends had substituted psychotherapeutic sessions for confession. Francis laments that so many people are going to diviners and fortunetellers. He suggests that this reveals that people want someone to talk to; someone who will listen to what is bothering them. He urges confessors to spend time with penitents, especially to listen to their stories. Francis calls this the "apostolate of the ear." I like that expression because it calls attention to how much good and healing can take place just by someone being an attentive and caring listener. I am looking forward to the next time I hear confessions.

Love Alone

Rereading Pope Francis, I think I have been reminded, or perhaps have seen in a deeper way, the mystery that surrounds the Sacrament of Reconciliation. Though it is more than fifty years ago, I remember the first time I heard confessions. I was nervous, but I think the predominant reaction that I had was a kind of awe or wonder. I have a similar awe and wonder as I reread Francis' insights into God's mercy.

One image that Francis offers of mercy is the wives

and mothers who line up in front of the jails on Saturdays and Sundays bringing food and presents to their husbands and sons. Noting that they do not disown their husbands and sons, Francis suggests that they show their love for them by undergoing the humiliation of being searched so that they can visit them. The Holy Father identifies it as a gesture of mercy. Though this may seem to us a small gesture, Francis believes it is not a small action to God.

Francis devotes a few pages to what he calls corruption. He claims that corruption is a sin which rather than being identified as such is elevated to a system and mental habit, actually a way of living. The corrupt person no longer feels the need for mercy but rather feels that he or she is justified and does not need forgiveness. The corrupt person does not repent. Francis writes the following:

> *"Sin, especially if repeated, can lead to corruption, not quantitatively—in the sense that a certain number of sins makes a person corrupt—but rather qualitatively: habits are formed that limit one's capacity for love and create a false sense of self-sufficiency. The corrupt man tires of asking for forgiveness and ends up believing that he doesn't need to ask for it anymore. We don't become corrupt people overnight, it is a long, slippery slope that cannot be identified simply as a series of sins . . . The corrupt man hides what he considers his true treasure, but which really makes him a slave and masks his vice with good manners, always managing to keep up appearances . . .*

> *"Corruption is not an act but a condition, a personal and social state in which we become accustomed to living. The corrupt man is so closed off and contented in the complacency of his self-sufficiency that he doesn't allow himself to be called into question by anything or anyone."* [75]

I hope I know myself well enough to be speaking the truth when I say that I am not the corrupt man. However, I hope I am humble enough to admit that I find aspects of myself in the description that Francis offers of the corrupt man. I am thinking of the Holy Father's insight that habits can be confirmed that limit one's capacity to love. Every sin is a sin against loving, but a habit of sins can make loving extremely difficult. Every sin is a movement toward selfishness and self-centeredness and that does not make loving more easy. Every choice of self over God, makes the next choice of self over God more easy.

In class at St. John's University, I frequently pose this question to the class: Can a person who repeatedly commits serious sins that break that person's relationship with God, still love his or her spouse? If a person has cut off relationship with God, can that person still have an unselfish loving relationship with a human being? For example, let us imagine a head of the Mafia who freely chooses to have people killed. Can such a person have a loving relationship with anyone? If he can, does this save him? Of course I don't know the answer to these questions, but the Holy Father's comments on the corrupt man has set me thinking about the effects of serious sin, not only on a person's rela-

---

[75] Ibid., p. 18.

tionship with God, but on the person's relationship with others.

It is not just serious sin, or mortal sin, that influences our capacity to love. All sin can make us less loving. What I think I must reflect on is the Holy Father's statement that we must avoid being content in our self-sufficiency. Eventually life shows us that we are not self-sufficient, but entering into a deeper love relationship with God must involve our freedom.

Discussion Questions

1. Do you agree that our refusal to forgive others blinds us to how much God forgives us?

2. Do you agree that the desire to be sorry for sins warrants absolution?

3. What is your experience of the Sacrament of Reconciliation? Why have the numbers of Catholics receiving the Sacrament reduced so dramatically?

4. Do you think that making a vow increases or decreases a person's freedom?

5. Is mercy the core of the Gospel message?

6. Do you think that a person who has rejected God is capable of loving anyone?

Conclusion

Personalist philosophers such as Martin Buber, Emmanuel Mounier, Gabriel Marcel and W. Norris Clarke, S.J. have given us wonderful insights into the mystery of human person and the mystery of God. Each thinker as he has probed into and reflected on the meaning of human person has unveiled for us something of the meaning and mystery of God. The deeper their reflections on human person, the deeper their awareness of God's love. Pope Francis has not presented insights into the human person and the mystery of God as a philosopher. Rather, his approach is entirely incarnational: he has urged us to live our relationships with one another, which will deepen not only our awareness of God but also our relationship with God. Pope Francis chose a wonderful quote from St. John of the Cross to end his book *The Name of God Is Mercy*. The quote is a perfect ending to Francis' book. I hope quoting Pope Francis' statement about St. John of the Cross is a fitting way to end this book as well:

> *"Let us always remember the words of St. John of the Cross: In the evening of our life, we will be judged on love alone."* [76]

---

[76] Ibid., p. 99

Additional Titles Published by Resurrection Press, a Catholic Book Publishing Imprint

A Rachel Rosary *Larry Kupferman*	$4.50
Blessings All Around Us *Dolores Leckey*	$8.95
Catholic Is Wonderful *Mitch Finley*	$4.95
The Dilemma of Divorced Catholics *John Catoir*	$8.95
Discernment *Chris Aridas*	$8.95
Feasts of Life *Jim Vlaun*	$12.95
Grace Notes *Lorraine Murray*	$9.95
Healing through the Mass *Robert DeGrandis, SSJ*	$9.95
Heart Peace *Adolfo Quezada*	$9.95
How Shall We Celebrate? *Lorraine Murray*	$6.95
How Shall We Pray? *James Gaffney*	$5.95
The Joy of Being an Altar Server *Joseph Champlin*	$5.95
The Joy of Being a Bereavement Minister *Nancy Stout*	$5.95
The Joy of Being a Catechist *Gloria Durka*	$4.95
The Joy of Being a Deacon *John P. Flanagan*	$6.95
The Joy of Being a Eucharistic Minister *Mitch Finley*	$5.95
The Joy of Being a Lector *Mitch Finley*	$5.95
The Joy of Pilgrimage *Lori Erickson*	$6.95
The Joy of Praying the Psalms *Nancy de Flon*	$5.95
The Joy of Praying the Rosary *James McNamara*	$5.95
The Joy of Preaching *Rod Damico*	$6.95
The Joy of Teaching *Joanmarie Smith*	$5.95
Lessons for Living from the 23rd Psalm *Victor Parachin*	$6.95
Lights in the Darkness *Ave Clark, O.P.*	$8.95
Loving Yourself for God's Sake *Adolfo Quezada*	$5.95
Meditations for Survivors of Suicide *Joni Woelfel*	$8.95
Mercy Flows *Rod Damico*	$9.95
More of Life and Love *Jim Lisante*	$9.95
Mother Teresa *Eugene Palumbo, S.D.B.*	$5.95
Mourning Sickness *Keith Smith*	$8.95
Our Grounds for Hope *Fulton J. Sheen*	$7.95
Pope Francis Spirituality *Robert E. Lauder*	$9.95
Praying the Lord's Prayer with Mary *Muto/vanKaam*	$8.95
5-Minute Miracles *Linda Schubert*	$4.95
Sabbath Moments *Adolfo Quezada*	$6.95
Sometimes I Haven't Got a Prayer *Mary Sherry*	$8.95
Womansoul *Pat Duffy, OP*	$7.95
You Are My Beloved *Mitch Finley*	$10.95

For a free catalog call 1-800-892-6657
www.catholicbookpublishing.com